PRAISE FOR *THE 4 DIMENSIONS OF EXTRAORDINARY LEADERSHIP*

"Leadership development is a lifelong pursuit and great leaders realize the need for resources to accompany them on the journey. In *The 4 Dimensions of Extraordinary Leadership*, Jenni Catron has created a leadership development tool that is structured enough to provide a guide, yet fluid enough to be a lifelong companion. Every leader at any stage will benefit from the truths presented in this book."

—JOHN C. MAXWELL, #1 *NEW YORK TIMES*
BESTSELLING AUTHOR AND LEADERSHIP EXPERT

"I have had the honor and privilege of working with church leaders around the world and across many denominations and sizes, and one of the things that I have discovered is just how crucial it is for leaders to be cultivating and raising up extraordinary leaders around them. In her new book, *The 4 Dimensions of Extraordinary Leadership*, Jenni Catron has established a framework for leadership development that is exceptional! If you are looking for a resource to help you grow your team, grow your leaders, and grow your influence to the world around you—this book is a must-read!"

—CHRISTINE CAINE, SPEAKER, AUTHOR OF *UNDAUNTED*,
AND FOUNDER OF THE A21 CAMPAIGN

"Leadership is never just a title and is always a lifestyle, an all-encompassing set of decisions that change the way you look at every facet of your life. I'm so glad that Jenni has captured that so succinctly in her own life and now in this great book!"

—JON ACUFF, *NEW YORK TIMES* BESTSELLING AUTHOR OF *DO OVER:*
RESCUE MONDAY, REINVENT YOUR WORK AND NEVER GET STUCK

"Leadership by its definition is lonely and complex, in *4 Dimensions* Jenni Catron gives great encouragement to leaders by breaking down the complexity and emphasizing the necessity of Christlike, God-centered leadership. This book is a great companion for anyone called to lead."

—ED STETZER, WWW.EDSTETZER.COM

"Jenni Catron creates a new framework for understanding leadership that aligns with God's command to love him with our whole heart, soul, mind, and strength. Through new and familiar stories about high-profile leaders, she highlights each aspect of their 'wholeness' and beautifully amplifies the gaps between ordinary and extraordinary leadership."

—TAMI HEIM, PRESIDENT AND CEO, CHRISTIAN LEADERSHIP ALLIANCE

"Many people complicate the magic of extraordinary leadership. Jenni Catron does an amazing job of simplifying what incredible leadership looks like. Not because it's easy, but because it's attainable to all who desire to be great leaders. You have to work at it and I'm so grateful Jenni is providing leaders a North Star to look at and pursue."

—TYLER REAGIN, EXECUTIVE DIRECTOR OF CATALYST

"Jenni Catron's latest book is a treasure chest full of wisdom on how to lead well . . . a must read for every leader. Both young leaders and more seasoned leaders will find insights, new perspectives, and encouragement."

—ALLI WORTHINGTON, EXECUTIVE DIRECTOR OF
PROPEL WOMEN AND AUTHOR OF *BREAKING BUSY*

"Straight from the heart of a gifted leader, Jenni Catron delivers a life-saving road map for leaders to live out all the dimensions of Jesus' great commandment to 'Love the Lord your God with all your heart, soul, mind, and strength.'"

—SANTIAGO "JIMMY" MELLADO, PRESIDENT AND
CEO, COMPASSION INTERNATIONAL

"While I believe that some people are naturally gifted to lead, great leadership still takes work. Jenni Catron is one of those people who is a super sharp leader *and* knows what it takes to grow and become an even better leader. Everyone who applies these leadership principles is guaranteed to see positive results."

—PERRY NOBLE, SENIOR PASTOR OF NEWSPRING CHURCH,
AUTHOR OF *UNLEASH!* AND *OVERWHELMED*

"Extraordinary leadership is possible when we consider *all* of the elements necessary to make it so. What Jenni has done in this remarkable book is just that . . . heart, soul, mind, and strength. She takes us on a deep dive in each of these four elements, then weaves them back together in to an integrated whole. Both her leadership experience and who she is as a person makes her uniquely gifted to write this book."

—Nancy Ortberg, CEO of Transforming the Bay with Christ

"Through her incredible experience and keen observations, Jenni offers unbelievable insights into leadership. If you have ever felt prompted to lead with all of who you are, then *The 4 Dimensions of Extraordinary Leadership* is a must read."

—Pete Wilson, pastor of Cross Point Church

"I get to work with some of the best leaders on the planet, and I will be recommending this book to each of them. Jenni takes lessons on leadership from ordinary life and lifts them into extraordinary teaching. A must read for growing leaders!"

—William Vanderbloemen, president of
Vanderbloemen Search Group

"Jenni Catron is one of my favorite leaders and it's fitting she's written a book on extraordinary leadership. Jenni models this and it is a gift to the rest of us to help understand her approach to serving and leading from these four dimensions. I am a better leader because of Jenni. I believe by reading this book you will be too."

—Jeff Henderson, lead pastor of Gwinnett Church

"As a leader of several fast-growing companies, I can tell you that Jenni Catron is the real deal. Her writings provide timeless truths that apply to leaders in any industry or organization. Jenni speaks from the heart, processes with her mind, leads with passion from her soul, and inspires with her strength. You will walk away from any encounter with Jenni—either in person or through her writings—a better leader than when you started."

—Shannon Miles, cofounder of eaHELP,
LLC, and MAG Bookkeeping, Inc.

"Should be required reading for anybody who wants to lead. This book gives a holistic approach on how to be a great leader that lasts the long-haul."

—Casey Graham, CEO, The Rocket Company

"*The 4 Dimensions of Extraordinary Leadership* is just that . . . extraordinary. This book is a road map on how to be a better leader. If you care at all about developing your gifts in leadership you need to read this book."

—Stephen Brewster, Creative Arts Pastor, Cross Point Church

"As anyone who has interacted with Jenni can sense, Jenni is a world-class leader. Drawing from her experience in the corporate world and from serving in two leading, progressive churches, Jenni shows you how to become the leader you've longed to become. This is a great book that will help many, many leaders."

—Carey Nieuwhof, lead pastor of Connexus Church, author, and blogger

"How do you define 'extraordinary leadership'? What qualities do extraordinary leaders have? How can you move from 'ordinary' to 'extraordinary'? Jenni Catron's must-read new book will help you discover your own answers and assist you in plotting your course from ordinary to extraordinary!"

—Bob Tiede, Cru Leadership Development Team and blogger @LeadingWithQuestions.com

"Jenni is no ordinary leader . . . She lives, loves, and leads wholeheartedly. She leads from her heart, soul, mind, and strength. You will be challenged and coached through this book by one of the very best."

—Jeanne Stevens, lead pastor, Soul City Church

THE 4 DIMENSIONS
OF EXTRAORDINARY
LEADERSHIP

THE 4 DIMENSIONS OF EXTRAORDINARY LEADERSHIP

*The Power of Leading from Your
Heart, Soul, Mind, and Strength*

Jenni Catron

NELSON
BOOKS

An Imprint of Thomas Nelson

Published in Nashville, Tennessee, by Nelson Books, an imprint of Thomas Nelson. Nelson Books and Thomas Nelson are registered trademarks of HarperCollins Christian Publishing, Inc.

Jenni Catron is represented by The Litton Group, a brand management and content strategy agency in Brentwood, Tennessee. Learn more at www.TheLittonGroup.com.

Thomas Nelson titles may be purchased in bulk for educational, business, fund-raising, or sales promotional use. For information, please e-mail SpecialMarkets@ ThomasNelson.com.

In some instances, names, dates, locations, and other identifying details have been changed to protect the identities and privacy of those mentioned in this book.

Unless otherwise noted, Scripture quotations are taken from the Holy Bible, New International Version®, NIV®. Copyright © 1973, 1978, 1984, 2011 by Biblica, Inc.® Used by permission of Zondervan. All rights reserved worldwide. www.zondervan.com. The "NIV" and "New International Version" are trademarks registered in the United States Patent and Trademark Office by Biblica, Inc.®

Scripture quotations marked ESV are from the ESV® Bible (The Holy Bible, English Standard Version®). Copyright © 2001 by Crossway, a publishing ministry of Good News Publishers. Used by permission. All rights reserved.

Scripture quotations marked KJV are from the King James Version. Public domain.

Scripture quotations marked THE MESSAGE are from The Message. Copyright © by Eugene H. Peterson 1993, 1994, 1995, 1996, 2000, 2001, 2002. Used by permission of Tyndale House Publishers, Inc.

Scripture quotations marked NASB are taken from New American Standard Bible®. Copyright © 1960, 1962, 1963, 1968, 1971, 1972, 1973, 1975, 1977, 1995 by The Lockman Foundation. Used by permission. (www.Lockman.org)

Scripture quotations marked NKJV are from the New King James Version®. © 1982 by Thomas Nelson. Used by permission. All rights reserved.

Library of Congress Cataloging-in-Publication Data

Catron, Jenni, 1976-
 The four dimensions of extraordinary leadership: the power of leading from your heart, soul, mind, and strength / Jenni Catron.
 pages cm
 Includes bibliographical references.
 ISBN 978–1–4002–0570–7
 1. Leadership—Religious aspects—Christianity. I. Title.
 BV4597.53.L43C4575 2015
 253—dc23
 2015004333

Printed in the United States of America

15 16 17 18 19 RRD 6 5 4 3 2 1

To my Nanny, a woman of strength and confidence.
Your tenacious spirit helped me believe anything
is possible. I love you and I miss you.

CONTENTS

CONTENTS

INTRODUCTION

The DNA of Extraordinary

I define leadership as an invitation to
greatness that we extend to others.[1]

—Mark Sanborn

Something about his leadership was different. I couldn't quite put my finger on it at first. It was difficult to identify. I had worked for a number of other leaders. Some of them were good, really good. But something still set Greg apart. He was an extraordinary leader. President of a thriving division of a corporation that was number one in its industry, he was at the pinnacle of his career. He had every reason to be brash, arrogant, and demanding, but instead he was kind, humble, and generous. He was succeeding and he understood why. Greg knew that all his accomplishments weren't possible without his team. He knew what many leaders miss: Leadership was not about him. It was about others. He understood that how he led others would affect the organization's continued success or failure. He realized his leadership mattered, and he seized every moment to lead like an extraordinary leader.

You know them when you see them. Extraordinary leaders. They stand out. They get your attention. It's not that they are always in the spotlight. That would be missing the point. Extraordinary leaders are faithfully leading in their places of influence, whether high profile or in seeming obscurity, but with such depth of purpose and sincere intentionality that has significant effects on those they lead.

Extraordinary leaders call others to their extraordinary best. They show up in all different types of settings. Like Greg, they can be seen in corporations. They show up in mom-and-pop businesses. They might be beloved football coaches or drama instructors. Vocation is irrelevant. Well-stewarded influence is the essential differential.

By definition, *extraordinary* means

Going beyond what is usual, regular, or customary
Exceptional to a very marked extent
Rare
Uncommon
Unique

Every one of these words and phrases makes me exclaim, "Yes, I want to be that!" I want to lead, guide, and direct others in a way that is unusual, exceptional, rare, uncommon, and unique.

I've experienced many less-than-extraordinary leaders, though. Haven't you? I've served under leaders who saw me only as a means to help them accomplish their goals. I've supported leaders who lacked the ability to make sound long-term decisions. I've been mistreated by seemingly soulless leaders who had little regard for the health of their staff. I've floundered under leaders who didn't really know where they wanted to go or leaders who changed their vision with each passing fad or popular idea. We've all served under an ordinary leader. Ordinary leadership is just that, ordinary. It's ordinary because it lacks purpose. It lacks a commitment to extraordinary. It lacks a passion to lead from a completely different paradigm.

What does extraordinary leadership look like? How do we become extraordinary leaders? What type of discipline is involved? What activities are necessary? What choices does one need to make? Why do people with great leadership instincts flounder?

These questions are difficult to sort out, and I know that it is a rare person who is a truly extraordinary leader. Great leadership is rare because it takes work. It takes intentionality. It requires sacrifice. It takes resolve. It involves heartaches, disappointments, and mistakes. It requires apologies. It entails a daily dose of humility. It means relentless growth and frequent failure.

Extraordinary leadership isn't easy, but it is possible. And when it emerges, it leads others to accomplish extraordinary things too.

What will it take? What does it look like? That's the expedition before us.

The Leader's Greatest Commandment

Leadership is hard. It's a difficult calling and responsibility. If I finish my life and haven't left a mark or made an impact that was significant to another person's life, I won't be content with that.

It's my "holy discontent," the term Pastor Bill Hybels has coined to describe the deep passion within us that moves us to make a difference. My holy discontent is to be an extraordinary leader. I want to jump out of my skin, inspired, when I see an extraordinary leader in action. I want to go into hiding and never emerge again when I fail remarkably in critical leadership moments. I want to study, learn, grow, and develop as a leader because I believe that great leadership is essential. It's necessary.

The search for extraordinary was born from this unquenchable passion to be a better leader. As I began to find myself in more and more leadership environments, I became increasingly aware of my inadequacies and inconsistencies as a leader. While I certainly had strengths that allowed me to lead in the first place, I also had some glaring deficiencies. I could either choose to mask my weakness or I could do some soul-searching and study great leaders to identify what was holding me back from truly being extraordinary.

While I quickly gravitated to studying the lives of historical leaders and biblical heroes, extraordinary emerged for me in the most common of these examples. Perhaps I thought I would discover this never-before-identified extraordinary leader who would radically change my view of leadership. I did find an example that radically changed my view of leadership, but I found it in one of the most foundational elements of my faith.

In the gospel of Mark, chapter 12, Jesus was being challenged with controversial questions about taxes and the resurrection. The final question posed to him was, "Which commandment is the most important of all?" (v. 28 ESV). Jesus responded with a fundamental biblical truth known as the Shema or more commonly understood as the Great Commandment: "Love the Lord your

God with all your heart and with all your soul and with all your mind and with all your strength" (v. 30). Then he proceeded to give those questioning him the second-greatest commandment: "Love your neighbor as yourself" (v. 31).

In Jewish tradition the Shema is recited three times a day as part of devotional life. According to the *Baker Encyclopedia of the Bible*, "Within the Shema is found both a fundamental doctrinal truth and a resultant obligation. There is an urgency connected to the teaching: the word *sh'ma* demands that the hearer respond with his total being to the fact and demands of this essential revelation."[2] Love God. Love others.

The Shema, or the Great Commandment, has enormous implications for us as leaders. This is where extraordinary is found. Within the Great Commandment is the model for extraordinary leadership. The more I've studied and read about leadership, the more formulas I've tried and the more strategies I've created, the more I've found my leadership theory keeps coming back to these original commandments of Jesus.

When Jesus asked us to love God with our heart, soul, mind, and strength, he was essentially saying that we should love God with all of ourselves—with everything in us. When he says love your neighbor as yourself, again the implication is to love with all of who you are. And so when I consider my life as a leader, it means leading with all of who I am for the benefit of God and others. Leadership requires all of me—my heart, my soul, my mind, and my strength. To not give all of me would be to shortchange God and others of what God has given me.

> **When I consider my life as a leader, it means leading with all of who I am for the benefit of God and others.**

We can't lead without our heart. We can't lead without our soul. We can't lead without our mind. We can't lead without our strength. We are integrated, messy, complicated humans, and when we learn that leading from all four of these dimensions is essential, we free ourselves to lead more fully.

And that's the point of this book. *The 4 Dimensions of Extraordinary Leadership* is a journey to unpack the four areas that I believe every leader must develop in order to lead extraordinarily.

Heart (Relational Leadership)

The heart of a leader is the truest part of who he or she is. Your heart is the center of your emotions, desires, and wishes. Your heart is what most connects you with others. "Love God. Love others" begins here in the heart. It's the relational dimension of leadership. Leading from the heart is about earning influence through relationships rather than authority. It's developing the art of emotional intelligence. When we lead from the heart, we see others as living, breathing humans with stories, emotions, families, strengths and weaknesses, and tragedies and joys. And when we see those we lead as human, we seek to relate with them through our God-given power to understand one another through emotional connection.

Soul (Spiritual Leadership)

The soul is the part of us that longs to know God. It's the epicenter of morality, integrity, humility, and servanthood. It is the spiritual component of our leadership and gives us the sensitivity to engage in the conversations that help lead people closer to God. It is the distinction that sets you apart as a faith-based leader.

Mind (Managerial Leadership)

The mind is the seat of intellectual activity. It is what enables us to deliberate, to process, to reflect, to ponder, and to remember. The mind enables us to strategize and to make plans. It is where we find clarity and where God imparts wisdom. The mind could also be viewed as the managerial component of leadership. Management is the method by which great leadership is executed. The mind enables us to take a leader's instincts and inspiration and put them into action. Leading with our minds allows us to make wise decisions about stewarding all the resources that God has entrusted to us. Management is the stewardship engine that drives leadership.

Strength (Visionary Leadership)

As leaders, we provide strength for our teams when we understand the power of vision. Those you lead must know that you deeply believe in where you're leading them and why. Winston Churchill's "keep calm and carry on" mantra provided consistent visionary leadership that enabled Britain to persevere against the Nazis in World War II. Visionary leadership means keeping hope and possibility in front of yourself and those you lead. It's recognizing that your job as a leader is chief vision caster every day.

From Ordinary to Extraordinary

Greg was an extraordinary leader because he understood that heart, soul, mind, and strength are essential. He knew he needed to lead himself well to lead us better. Although he was at the top of his career, he knew he hadn't personally arrived. There was more to learn and more to do. There were more ways to grow, and he positioned himself to do just that.

Greg was well loved by our team because he put his whole heart into it. He understood relational leadership. He knew our names, our interests, our families, and our hobbies. Honestly, I'm not sure how he kept up with it all, but I believe it was because he truly cared. People were important to him, and he made a point of making sure all employees knew they mattered.

Spiritual leadership was a significant and unique part of Greg's story. Ironically, he had originally taken a job as the warehouse manager for this tiny company to make money to put himself through seminary. Greg had every intention of being a student pastor, yet fifteen years later he found himself at the helm of a multimillion-dollar corporation. While Greg didn't pray at every meeting, his spiritual leadership spoke loudly through how he conducted himself and how he interacted with staff. He did indeed create a time of weekly staff devotions, and I was privy to the circumstances that would often lead him to prayer.

Greg led with his mind and managed us well. He didn't shy away from giving feedback—good *and* bad. A job well done was well celebrated. A poor decision was met with encouragement to do better next time. I always knew where I stood in regard to my performance on the team, and as a result I could proceed confidently. I knew I would be coached for success.

Greg always reminded us of the purpose behind everything we did. He knew that his title of president really meant "chief vision caster." He knew we could get lost in the details, and it was his job to remind us of the possibilities ahead.

Greg wasn't superhuman. He was an ordinary guy wrestling the demands of his everyday life, but he chose to center his leadership on the Great Commandment. Greg displayed the everyday actions of an extraordinary leader. And you can too.

Together we'll look at what it means to be a leader. What are the conflicting definitions, and how can we bring clarity to them? We'll look at the complexity of leadership and its inherent demands. We'll unpack each dimension of leadership and help you identify possible gaps in your leadership development. We'll consider examples of leading from heart, soul, mind, and strength and give you steps to lead more holistically from all four. Then we'll put it all together and make sense of what living like an extraordinary leader looks like in our sphere of influence. Finally, we'll conclude with what it looks like to lead others to be extraordinary leaders too.

I believe you can be extraordinary! I believe you have the potential to develop in heart, soul, mind, and strength and live out your leadership in ways that truly change the trajectory of not only your life but also the lives of those you lead. It's a heavy calling, a weighty responsibility. But I believe every leader has the potential to go from ordinary to extraordinary. You aspire to be a leader because you want to make a difference, you want to influence change, and you want to make a mark. Here's your chance. I believe you can!

Questions for Reflection

- Is there someone in your life who has modeled extraordinary leadership?
- What set him or her apart as an extraordinary leader?
- What do you think it will take for you to become an extraordinary leader too?

PART 1

FROM
ORDINARY TO
EXTRAORDINARY

Embedded in the larger story
of redemption is a principle we
must not miss: God uses ordinary
people to do extraordinary
things in the lives of others.[1]

—Paul David Tripp

CHAPTER 1

IMAGINE EXTRAORDINARY

> The challenge of leadership is to be strong, but not
> rude; be kind, but not weak; be bold, but not bully; be
> thoughtful, but not lazy; be humble, but not timid; be
> proud, but not arrogant; have humor, but without folly.[1]
>
> **—Jim Rohn**

W hat is your new job, Jenni?"

"I'm the shared resources leader at Menlo Church."

"What exactly do you do?"

And right about there is where the conversation gets stuck. I can't begin to explain the strained expressions and confused looks my new title has caused people in the last months. In March 2014, I made a major career leap from executive director at Cross Point Church in Nashville, Tennessee, to join the central leadership team at Menlo Church in Menlo Park, California.

It was a big move in a number of ways—emotionally, physically, culturally—you name it, we experienced it. My husband and I were well loved by friends and family, who supported us and encouraged us through the transition. We frequently addressed questions about the move date, when we'd visit again, where we'd be living, and so on, but then I'd often get one more question: "So, what *exactly* is it you'll be doing?" Repeatedly people would be tripped up by the new title: "shared resources leader." The function of my new job was actually very similar to the role I'd had at Cross Point, but the title gave people very little context to understand it.

Puzzled by how frequently I received that question, I began to wonder what it was about the title that made it feel so vague. Then it dawned on me that the key word in my title was not *manager* or *director*; it was *leader*. Our corporate cultures and hierarchies have conditioned us to know how to position these more common titles, but the word *leader* is vague. Although the word has many definitions, it is difficult to pin down the concepts of leaders and leadership.

"What does leadership mean to you?" The number of times I've been asked that question is exasperating. And the number of times I couldn't answer it or fumbled over flimsy definitions and half-baked arguments is even more irritating.

What is leadership? The term could benefit from a redefinition, couldn't it? The subject of leadership evokes angst, opposition, elitism, skepticism, fear, and favor. People who aren't leaders often claim to be. Strong leaders often run from accepting leadership. Those afraid of authority revolt against those in leadership positions.

I understand the tension. I can't help but cringe at some of the ways the word *leadership* gets used.

We diminish the word's power when we argue that everyone

is a leader because everyone leads someone. I understand this definition. I don't completely disagree with it, but it's not exactly complete. I would clarify it: we all have *influence* with others, but that doesn't necessarily make you a great leader. Leadership begins with influence. But leadership isn't simply influence.

We don't refer to the tyrants of history as leaders, but if our definition of leadership is simply influence, then horrific people like Adolf Hitler are leaders. If in my aspiration to become a leader, I'm going to find my name among the ranks of a Nazi terror, no thank you. I'll move on and do something different. I want to aspire to something great. I want to make a difference, leave a mark. I want to influence people's lives—for good. If the continuum of leadership runs the gamut from Adolf Hitler to Mother Teresa, our definition is too broad. It's cumbersome. We lack common language, and therefore we lack focus in understanding what it means to be a leader.

I believe that at its core, the word *leadership* is an observation of greatness. Leadership is rarely observable in the moment, but it is recognizable in outcomes. In the book *Greatness*, Steven F. Hayward says, "Typically we only recognize greatness in hindsight."[2] Additionally, he writes, "Greatness is not purely circumstantial. Greatness is ultimately a question of character. Good character does not change with the times: it has eternal qualities."[3] That thought resonates with the spirit of leading from our heart, soul, mind, and strength, doesn't it? Great leadership is an action; it's a lifestyle. A lifestyle of leading from our whole selves—heart, soul, mind, and strength.

In an article titled "What Is Leadership?," *Forbes* contributor Kevin Kruse wrestles with some of the popular definitions of leadership:

*"The only definition of a leader is someone
who has followers."* —Peter Drucker

*"Leadership is the capacity to translate
vision into reality."* —Warren Bennis

*"As we look ahead into the next century, leaders
will be those who empower others."* —Bill Gates

*"Leadership is influence—nothing more,
nothing less."* —John Maxwell

Kruse argues that these definitions are incomplete, and he provides his own: "Leadership is a process of social influence, which maximizes the efforts of others, towards the achievement of a goal."[4]

Kruse's definition is a strong one. It takes into account the importance of influence rather than position or authority; it entails the mobilization of others toward a goal. It suggests employing relational (heart) equity to help others catch your vision (strength) and manage (mind) them to help accomplish the goal. Soul is obviously lacking in this definition. And there is one more thing Kruse's definition omits, something I believe is essential for extraordinary leaders. Before we can lead others from our heart, soul, mind, and strength, there is a key first step. I believe it is the starting point of leadership. To lead others well, we must first lead ourselves better.

To lead others well, we must first lead ourselves better.

Extraordinary leaders learn to lead themselves first. They develop the discipline to understand their motivations, to continually evaluate their emotional health, to manage their physical health, and to nurture their spiritual life. From the overflow of their understanding of themselves, leaders can then focus on the priority of leadership: leading others.

As we discuss the dimensions of an extraordinary leader, I hope to inspire you to embrace this definition of leadership:

Extraordinary leadership is found in a leader who has searched to discover his or her authentic self and from that place influences others to accomplish great dreams through intentional relationships (heart), spiritual awareness (soul), wise counsel (mind), and relentless vision (strength).

Learning to live out this definition is the journey that we're going to take together. Now that we have an idea of what leadership is, we need to understand where leadership begins.

Before we dig too deep, I want to invite you to take an assessment I've created to help you diagnose where you are right now. Understanding where we are in our leadership journey equips us to develop a plan for where we want to go. This assessment will give you an idea of where you are naturally strong as a leader and help you define the areas that will enable you to grow into the extraordinary leader you desire to be. Moving from ordinary to extraordinary is a progression, not an overnight process. Extraordinary is a result of a hungry, teachable attitude and a commitment to consistent growth and progress.

Extraordinary Leadership Assessment

To start, read the statements below and circle the ones you most identify with. Try not to spend time analyzing the statements; instead, respond with your initial instinct. Be honest with yourself, and circle only the statements that describe who you are today—not the statements that describe who you would like to be.

 I subscribe to blogs and e-mail newsletters that explore my industry, and I like to read them daily.

 When meeting with an employee, I first like to hear about his or her family and how he or she is doing personally.

 I pray for my team members regularly.

 I believe wholeheartedly in the vision of my organization.

 I plan regular events or outings to celebrate my team members and let them know they're appreciated.

 I set goals with and for my team members and create follow-up plans to measure the results.

 When my schedule for the day starts to get out of hand, I stop, look at it, and quickly prioritize, turning down or rescheduling the non-urgent tasks.

 When deadlines are looming, I tend to focus more on the tasks that need to be accomplished than the people doing the tasks.

I avoid gossip, complaints, and criticism in my daily speech and conversations.

 I regularly let my team members know that they are valuable to our organization and their work is essential to the mission.

 I know my strengths and like to focus on working in those areas while delegating the items I'm not as strong at.

 I'm always looking for opportunities to connect my team's everyday work to the big picture of our vision and to share that connection with my team.

 I'm good at defining systems and strategies and holding my team accountable to them.

 I seek opportunities to encourage those I lead by praising them and giving them feedback to help them develop further.

 I pray for wisdom for my team members so that they will grow in influence.

 I judge my success as a leader by how well I'm serving my team.

 I feel stronger at painting the big picture than fleshing out the minute details.

I devote time to meeting with a mentor or group of people who are ahead of me and who help stretch my thinking and challenge me.

 I want my team members to know that they are loved and that they can talk to me about anything.

 My leadership position is not just a job to me—it's where I live out my strongest convictions, passions, and hopes for the future.

 I regularly take stock of my spiritual growth.

 I sometimes get distracted by worrying if my leaders or team members like me.

 If I don't know how to do something, I do research and learn how to do it or I assign it to someone who knows how to do it.

 I feel a great responsibility to God for how I lead my team and pray for his guidance daily.

 I am always dreaming up new ideas for building my team/business and can't wait to implement them.

 It frustrates me if I'm not able to communicate to my team members the "heart" behind a decision I've made that affects them.

I believe my spiritual health has a direct effect on my leadership ability.

 I regularly review my team's meeting structure to see which meetings are necessary and to ensure we're making the most of our time and resources.

Now tally the number of statements you circled for each symbol/dimension of leadership.

Which dimension (or two) did you most identify with? These are the areas where you are probably naturally strong as a leader. The dimensions you didn't identify with as much are the areas with room for growth. Keep these results in mind as you continue reading.

Where Do Leaders Come From?

Christine was born to lead. From the day she could talk, she began bossing her siblings around. On Saturday afternoons she could be found rallying the neighborhood kids for a game of kickball or organizing a quest to capture butterflies. In school she easily excelled and was consistently at the top of her class while also donning the titles of homecoming queen and student body president. She was gregarious and charming, smart and strong. People followed her with ease, and her influence didn't slow down throughout college and into her career. If ever a leader appeared to be a natural, it was Christine.

There is an ongoing debate in schools of leadership theory as to whether leaders are born or made. It's leadership's version of the chicken or the egg conundrum. Are you born with the ability to lead or is leadership something you develop?

I believe it's both. You *can* be born with a natural propensity, an innate wiring to be a great leader, much like Christine was. Potential leaders are born with natural instincts and personality traits that equip them for leadership, but I also believe that leadership has to be developed. Without development, that gift could remain idle or, worse, be misused. A key part of Christine's story is that although she showed early signs of leadership, it was the intentionality of her parents, teachers, and mentors that helped foster her natural leadership strengths and enabled her to thrive and grow.

You become a leader when you develop the skills and the competence to put that influence into action.

While some are born with leadership instincts, others find themselves placed into positions of leadership whether they're naturally gifted for it or not. That was certainly the case with Greg, the leader we discussed in the introduction. While he was obviously born with leadership instincts, he was thrown into the deep end of the leadership pool when he found himself heading up a company he had not aspired to lead. He was placed in a position of leadership that exceeded his experience to that point.

Some are born with leadership gifts. Others are placed into positions of leadership. But whether you are a born leader or have been placed into leadership, you will not automatically develop into a great leader. These opportunities have simply given you the influence to lead. You become a leader when you develop the skills and the competence to put that influence into action. I wholeheartedly believe that with focus and intentionality you can grow and develop into a great leader.

A *Fast Company* article says this:

> The first thing Tom Kolditz wants you to know about leaders is that most of them didn't emerge from diapers to direct teams naturally. "If you look at the research done, the qualities leaders were born with, [such as] intelligence and attractiveness, account for 30 percent of leadership," says the retired brigadier general, who spent the last 12 years of his career running the leadership program he developed at the U.S. Military Academy at West Point.
>
> "What that means is that 70 percent is learned—from your parents or the school of hard knocks or leader development programs. That's a big part that is malleable and attainable through training," he says.[5]

While there is a certain element of leadership that may be imparted to us, those of us who aspire to grow as leaders must cultivate our growth. To really develop as a leader takes teaching and coaching. In that way, you could argue that leaders are made. Great leadership doesn't just magically happen. We have to study, learn, pray, and keep at it, learning from every circumstance and opportunity.

What Do We Do with It?

Accept the Responsibility of Leadership

Extraordinary leaders know that their leadership gifts and abilities are not for their own benefit. The gift of leadership is a gift to you to give to others. Extraordinary leaders are other-centric. They recognize that leadership at its core is an act of service. It's living out the second half of the Great Commandment: Love God. *Love others.*

The influence we earn as leaders is not for the purpose of wielding power. It's for the purpose of loving others enough to help them develop and use their gifts. It's for rallying a group of people to accomplish an audacious goal. It's for helping others realize their dreams. It's for calling others to growth and improvement in ways that motivate and inspire them to do their best.

Jesus modeled the responsibility of leadership in the way he engaged with his disciples in everyday life. From washing their feet in an act of humility and service, to directing them to feed the thousands, to sharing quiet times of prayer and reflection, to painting the picture of their responsibility once he was gone, Jesus loved and led his disciples with the purpose of helping them grow and develop. It wasn't about him; it was about them.

Keep Your Eye on the Big Picture

If you want to be an extraordinary leader, your greatest challenge and responsibility is to keep your eye on the big picture. You must be the proverbial plate spinner, being attentive to every aspect of the organization, sensitive to each person you lead, aware of the implications of each decision you make, and balancing the numerous priorities that come your way. In addition to the obvious responsibilities, you also must attend to the dimensions that will help you succeed as a leader: heart, soul, mind, and strength.

Two or three of these dimensions will probably come easily to you. You'll naturally excel and prioritize them into the flow of your work. However, a couple of these will also repeatedly trip you up. When you are under stress, the ones that are most difficult for you will fall by the wayside, and the ones at which you excel will become overused. For instance, I'm naturally strong in tactics and planning, attributes of the mind dimension of the leader. Under stress I will dig into managing anything and everything I can. The more my mind works, the more competent I feel. But stress turns my managerial strengths into micromanagement and impatience. When details are not attended to as quickly or as thoroughly as I prefer, I become tense and demanding.

During a particularly busy Christmas season, the team that I was working with was also understaffed. Tensions were high and the days were long. As our Christmas events approached, the intensity ramped up and my communication became terser. After a series of tense conversations with one of my staff members, I realized that I was being completely insensitive and had to stop to apologize and repair the relationship.

Relational leadership, which is a dimension that I have to work at more intentionally, becomes nonexistent to me when deadlines are looming. Because of my task-oriented nature, I see the work that needs to be done before seeing the people who are doing it. I can easily lose the heart dimension in my leadership.

As you read this book, study the dimensions and assess yourself on them. Begin to pay attention to which ones come naturally and how these show up in your everyday leadership. Also look for where your weaker dimensions become nonexistent. You're on your way to extraordinary leadership when you learn to keep all the dimensions spinning consistently. I believe *leader*, by definition, means great. Exceptionally great. Counterculturally great. Revolutionarily great. And you have the potential to be just that!

Questions for Reflection

- How do you define leadership?
- Based on the assessment, which dimension is your strongest? Which is your weakest?
- What is one thing you could do this week to focus your leadership on others?

CHAPTER 2

LEADING IN CHAOS

Leaders live and lead in the middle of the mess. Where
the tension is constant, prevalent, and real.[1]

—Brad Lomenick

I was in my early twenties at the starting gate of my career. A couple of years of loyal hard work had earned me a promotion, and I was extremely proud that I was going to be responsible for managing another employee.

It didn't take long before I found myself exasperated because my new wonderful employee wasn't doing things exactly the way I thought she should or the way I had instructed her.

As a type A, dominant achiever, and now a first-time manager, I was *any* employee's living nightmare. I, of course, thought I was her greatest gift.

My new employee wasn't meeting my expectations, so in my frustration I went to my boss, the VP and a mentor in my life, for counsel. But rather than nod in agreement and share my frustration, he said something to me that frankly just made me mad. He said, "Jenni, you're working with people not widgets. If you want things to be perfect and go exactly your way, you're in the wrong business."

I wasn't particularly fond of his feedback. I had walked into his office convinced my employee was the problem, but my boss was quick to point out that it wasn't my employee—it was *me*. The problem lay with *my* perspective. I was expecting leadership to be simple and streamlined, to align with my neat and tidy ideals. I was envisioning an assembly line of "people-widgets" carrying out my every instruction without applying their thoughts, ideas, gifts, or experiences. I wanted a simple and controllable dictatorship, not leadership. That early lesson was a defining point in my leadership life. Without realizing it, I was presented with the choice to lead from the second part of the Great Commandment: love others. In my pomp and arrogance I was making leadership about me.

That experience was my first memorable introduction to the idea that leadership is a very complex issue. It's not an assembly line of widgets responding to my every beck and call. It's not clearly definable and controllable outcomes. It's not well-conceived plans that never fail. It's not circumstances that I can always control.

> **Leadership is all about people, and people are complex.**

Leadership is messy, murky, complicated, and rarely black-and-white. Leadership is all about people, and people are complex.

The Tension of Leadership

Have you ever found yourself in a situation where the answer just wasn't clear? Maybe it was a decision to take a new job in a different city. Maybe it was a really confusing or inconsistent relationship. Maybe it was taking a risk that didn't seem to have a clear reward.

Have you ever found yourself frustrated with all the decisions you have to make as a leader?

I think we would all agree that there is little about life that is easy to navigate. We face tough decisions every single day. And as a leader, you're not only facing your own decisions but navigating the decision making for your entire team and organization.

Jessica was tasked with a turnaround situation. The challenges facing the company were complicated. It was stable and profitable and seemingly doing fine with the status quo. Jessica's task was to help the senior leadership see the untapped potential that she believed they could achieve, while also painting a picture of the dangers of the unknown if they didn't make some changes for the future. The company wasn't necessarily feeling any pain under its current mode of operation, but Jessica's instincts told her it was just a matter of time before it would.

Leaders live in a constant state of tension. Like Jessica, we live between what is and what could be. We straddle the known and the unknown. We wrestle the probable with the possible. We balance status quo with innovation. We have to understand where we are yet convince our teams to keep going.

There are numerous tensions great leaders navigate each and every day. And living with these tensions is a tension in and of itself. This constant tug and pull stretches you to either expand and grow or snap under the stress.

If you're anything like me, sometimes you find yourself frustrated with the complexity you face. Have you ever said things like, "Couldn't leadership be easier for just one day? Could I please have a day when I don't need to make a decision?"

But if all of life were clear shades of black or white—if there were no difficult decisions to be made—there would be no need for leaders. That's the game-changing reality for us. The great tension and the great responsibility of leadership means navigating the complexity our circumstances present. That's what we do. It's who we are. The willingness to engage the tension is what separates us from the pack. It's what begins to define us as leaders.

These tensions of leadership fascinate me because I believe there is so much that we can learn from them. But if I'm honest, they also really frustrate me. In studying that frustration I've learned that identifying and naming these tensions allows me to see them as part of my leadership growth rather than a nuisance to avoid. I don't think the tensions ever go away either. Leading through these tensions is at the heart of what we do as leaders.

The very purpose of leadership is to effectively navigate the tensions facing ourselves, our organizations, and our staffs. What I know to be true is that leaders emerge most prominently when things are confusing and chaotic. Often this is referred to as a "leadership vacuum." Deepak Chopra, author of *War of the Worldviews* and founder of the Chopra Foundation, shares his observations about this phenomenon in a *Huffington Post* article titled "The Leadership Vacuum—Make It Your Friend":

When a leadership vacuum appears, there's stress. Chaos threatens to erupt. It would seem that only a unique person, someone whose chemistry mixes ambition, charisma, and ego, can fill the vacuum. But when teaching an approach I call "the soul of leadership," I begin with the opposite assumption, that leaders appear when awareness meets need. A person who knows what a group actually needs—the group can be a family, business, team, or political party—must be more aware than those in need. If they had enough awareness on their own, the leadership vacuum wouldn't persist. Once the need is identified, the leader must take steps to fill the role that it demands.[2]

Knowing what a group actually needs is the crux of the complexity leaders face. Leaders must wade through the confusing circumstances, navigate relational tensions, and lead themselves and others to hope and possibility. It's a complex task but a remarkable privilege. That's what extraordinary leaders do.

Leading Through Tension

James Burke, once at the helm of the leading company in his industry, now found himself staring down his greatest nightmare: market share was plummeting, millions of dollars were on the line, and a media frenzy was building. Seven people had died after taking cyanide-laced extra-strength Tylenol capsules. As CEO of Johnson & Johnson, Burke had to lead through this crisis, most assuredly facing the greatest tension he had experienced as a leader. A *Time* article recounts the story:

According to media reports at the time, the Tylenol crisis led the news every night on every station for six weeks. Burke, however, met the challenge head on, contacting the chief of each network's news divisions in order to keep them informed. He also met with the directors of the FBI and the

FDA. "There were many people in the company who felt there was no possible way to save the brand, that it was the end of Tylenol," Burke said. "But the fact is, I had confidence in J&J and its reputation, and also confidence in the public to respond to what was right. It helped turn Tylenol into a billion-dollar business.[3]

Much like every crisis, the Tylenol crisis was screaming for extraordinary leadership. There was a desperate need for a leader to provide strength, clarity, and confidence both for the public and for the employees of Johnson & Johnson. While his position dictated that Burke was the leader, his actions firmly established him as the leader. Burke understood that leading through the complexity of that situation required heart, soul, mind, and strength. His legacy of leadership led *Fortune* magazine to name him in 2003 as one of history's ten greatest CEOs.[4]

Burke and the Tylenol crisis give us a glimpse of what leading from heart, soul, mind, and strength look like in action.

Heart

Burke displayed heart by connecting with the emotions of his customers. He understood that fear and doubt were powerful forces in people's lives. He recognized that people were going to need him to take ownership and to take action.

One of the tensions that leaders face in crisis involves their willingness to engage their own emotions and those of others. Often leaders will ignore their emotions to stay focused on dealing with an issue. While compartmentalizing our own emotions may help us focus and take action, we can actually lose credibility if we appear less than human. Those we lead need to know that we feel and understand the emotions of the situation. Burke found a healthy balance of caring and connecting while assertively responding.

Soul

Burke also didn't neglect his soul in this leadership crisis. He owned responsibility and acted with moral integrity. He was honest, forthright, and sincere in his response. He didn't attempt to hide or manipulate circumstances. Burke demonstrated what Mark Miller describe in his book *The Heart of Leadership*: "It's our leadership character that ultimately drives what we do, and why. It is a true reflection of who we really are as human beings."[5] Burke earned trust in the middle of an extreme crisis because he led with integrity.

Mind

Burke owned his responsibility to bring clarity and direction to the situation. He understood that confusion always hinders momentum. And as leaders, we need to passionately protect momentum. Leadership expert John Maxwell expresses it this way: "As a leader, your responsibility is to understand momentum, to get it moving for your organization, and to sustain it over time."[6] When something is hindering momentum, a leader must take notice. Too much is at stake. A leader's job is to make sense of confusion. You need to provide clarity and to create a clear next step, a clear path for those you lead. Burke displayed the mind of a leader by seeking the wisdom to bring clarity to the situation and provide a plan of response.

Strength

When tensions abound, people are looking for strength. Strength in wisdom. Strength of character. They are looking for a leader who is able to convey that "it's going to be okay." They want someone who projects hope and possibility even in the face of uncertainty.

Burke verbalized his confidence even in the midst of doubt. He reassured his people and the public that J&J would be the company it claimed to be. The integrity of its brand was at stake, and he confidently declared his commitment to be faithful to its mission of serving its customers first. According to the *Time* article quoted earlier, "Under Burke's leadership, the company spent $100 million to recall 31 million bottles of Tylenol and re-launched the product two months later in tamper-proof packaging."[7] These actions gave consumers confidence to reengage with the brand.

When we as leaders face a complex problem or crisis, we must consider our responsibility to display heart, soul, mind, and strength. Before we can lead others well, we have to settle these needs for ourselves.

Undoubtedly, strong is the last thing you feel when a challenge is looming larger than life. But you must gather strength from wise counselors, mentors, and friends. If you're a person of faith, your foundation for strength resides in your assurance in God's provision and protection.

While running to take action may be your natural inclination, an extraordinary leader will pause to get clarity on the situation. What are the facts? What are the present circumstances? What additional information do you need? Pause to think through the situation and your plan of action. You must have a clear plan in mind to provide clarity for others. You don't have to have the entire plan mapped out, but be certain to pause to determine the appropriate next step.

Remind yourself of what is true of you, the team, and the vision. Reengage with the big picture and overarching purpose, and then confidently remind others. Your hopefulness and confidence will allow those you lead to feel confident too.

Heart, Soul, Mind, and Strength— and Complexity

One of my favorite extraordinary leaders in the Bible is Nehemiah. In the Old Testament book named for him, Nehemiah led the Jewish people to rebuild the wall of Jerusalem that had lain in shambles for seventy years. While the Jewish people had returned to Jerusalem to rebuild the temple after some fifty years of exile, they were never able to finish the wall around the temple. It was left in ruin because they faced opposition each time they attempted to complete it. No leader before Nehemiah had the clarity of vision and the influence to overcome obstacles to accomplish this monumental task.

What's striking about Nehemiah's story is that he wasn't personally affected by the wall. He didn't live in Jerusalem. Nehemiah was in Judea serving as the cupbearer to the king of Persia. This was a high-profile position. He had earned a respected seat of influence, so the fact that he was concerned about the people in his homeland speaks volumes about his character.

As you read through his story, you quickly see that Nehemiah understood the complexity of the leadership task before him. He recognized that there was a problem to solve and that no one else was stepping up to solve it. He identified the leadership vacuum that existed, and he felt called to help lead through it. As we look at Nehemiah's actions, we see how he employed the dimensions of an extraordinary leader to lead himself and others through the complexity of the problem they faced.

He Identified the Problem

After spending a few days in Jerusalem assessing the situation, Nehemiah told the other leaders, "You see the trouble we are in: Jerusalem lies in ruins, and its gates have been burned with fire. Come, let us rebuild the wall of Jerusalem, and we will no longer be in disgrace" (Nehemiah 2:17). The first task of the leader is to define reality, especially when a complex problem lies between where you are and where you desire to go. In Nehemiah's case, it was a wall that lay in ruins, and those ruins symbolized a lack of hope, a lack of strength, and a lack of direction for God's people. He was burdened. Nehemiah owned it. It was personal.

He Sought Out Support (Heart)

Nehemiah knew he couldn't do this alone. He needed others to help him accomplish the vision of restoring the wall. Nehemiah's role as cupbearer to the king was no accident. He strategically used his place of influence to petition the king for permission to take a leave of absence from his job to lead the rebuilding effort. In addition, he asked the king to write letters to other government officials from whom he would need help.

In each step of the process, Nehemiah cast vision and began recruiting help: first to the officials, then to the priests, and finally to the citizens of Jerusalem. He engaged and involved people at every level, and Scripture says that "the people worked with all their heart" (Nehemiah 4:6).

He Prayed over It (Soul)

Nehemiah displayed spiritual leadership by praying for God to give him direction for how to proceed. According to *Halley's Bible Handbook*, "He spent four months in prayer before he made his request to the king,"[8] and Scripture cites numerous times when he paused to pray throughout the project. And these weren't puny prayers. Nehemiah 1:4 tells us that Nehemiah wept, mourned, fasted, and prayed before the God of heaven. When was the last time your heart hurt like that on behalf of someone else?

He Developed a Plan (Mind)

Upon arriving in Jerusalem, Nehemiah visited the remnants of the wall and outlined a plan for rebuilding. He took his plan to the city officials and received their blessing, thanks in large part to the letters from King Artaxerxes. With permission to build, Nehemiah recruited the workers. He provided clear direction and regular guidance, especially when they faced challenges. When opposition arose, he posted guards day and night. When the laborers grew fatigued because of the threats of attack, Nehemiah created rotations so that their responsibilities and the associated pressures would vary. Nehemiah's attentiveness to the details of the process and the implications of the work for the people exemplified his awareness of managerial leadership.

He Saw the Possibility (Strength)

Nehemiah developed a personal passion for this problem, and from that passion a vision of hope for the future was born. While he identified a problem, he also caught a vision for the possibilities. The fact that Nehemiah developed this vision on behalf of others is significant. He didn't see the possibilities as a benefit for himself. He saw the possibilities for others. Amidst criticism, threats on his life, grumbling from those he was seeking to help, and the difficulties of the task, Nehemiah stayed the course and displayed unwavering commitment to the vision God gave him. His selfless leadership showcased the strength of an extraordinary leader.

Embracing the Tension

What gives leaders like Nehemiah the courage to lead through a seemingly impossible obstacle? How do you muster the moxie to take on a task that others have shied away from or failed at? How do you embrace the tension between possibility and the fear of the unknown?

In their book, *The Leadership Pipeline: How to Build the Leadership-Powered Company*, Ram Charan, Stephen Drotter, and James Noel argue that leaders need to be aware of the passages they must go through in their development, specifically as they climb the ranks within an organization. Passage six leads to the highest level of most organizations, and the authors assert that it's here where the transition is "much more focused on values than skills." They go on to say, "As leaders of an institution, [managers] must be long-term, visionary thinkers. At the same time, they must develop operating mechanisms to know and drive quarter-by-quarter performance that is in tune with longer-term strategy."[9]

In essence, the authors are explaining the tension that leaders must embrace to effectively lead with increased levels of responsibility. Extraordinary leaders understand that they have to think differently and think on behalf of the entire organization rather than only the portion for which they're specifically responsible.

When we fully embrace the reality that complexity is our playing field as leaders, it becomes a game changer for how we approach our leadership. We no longer see complexity as a frustration. We see it as an opportunity. Complexity is where our best leadership happens. We see the potential to which we get to lead our teams. Part of being a leader is being able to see what's on the other side of the complexity. As a leader, you have a vision for the outcome and you lead your team confidently through the haze.

Take the First Step

Embracing the tensions of leadership means being willing to go first. It requires the bravery of a first step. I think of the priests who were carrying the ark of the covenant and were about to cross the Jordan River. God had promised that the waters would part so they could cross over to the promised land, yet it wasn't until their feet touched the water's edge that the river stopped flowing and they were able to cross (Joshua 3:15–16). Joshua and the priests had to be willing to go first. They had to be willing to be one step ahead.

Complexity is where our best leadership happens.

When we as leaders choose to take the first step, those we lead can see our confidence and faith. We can't rush ahead or get impatient. We must give guidance and coach passionately. Extraordinary leaders lead through the tension. They don't get lost in it. They don't get bogged down by it. They push through it to find clarity and provide the next step for others.

On numerous occasions I have worked with teams that have had a tendency to get paralyzed by their desired outcome. Because it feels so far from reality, they quickly get discouraged by their perceived inability to get from where they are today to where they hope to be in the future. Recently one of the ministry teams that I worked with several years ago posted pictures from an event. Hundreds of people participated in an event that was only a dream when we first began working through the challenges that were impeding the growth we longed for. They didn't arrive at today's reality overnight. It came through focus, dedication, and a commitment from their leader to take it step by step, celebrating every little win along the way.

Face Your Fears

Embracing the tensions of leadership doesn't mean we don't face fear. In the complexity we face some of our greatest fears—fear of inadequacy, fear of failure, fear of criticism.

Often the difference between success and stagnation is confronting a fear. Author and Bible teacher Jennie Allen confronted a series of personal fears when she stepped out to launch IF, an organization whose purpose is to gather, equip, and unleash the next generation of women to live out their purpose. Jennie felt that God was calling her to start this gathering, yet everything within her wanted to retreat out of fear. If Jennie had not embraced the tension of fear in her life, she wouldn't have experienced IF's current success. With its first event, IF connected with more than 150,000 women worldwide. Because she faced her fears, tens of thousands of lives have been affected.

You must face your fears. You must choose to face the loneliness of being the only one who sees the potential clearly. You must fight through. You must push through so you can lead others through. And once you lead them through the tension, you will have the privilege of seeing your team experience the joy of a clear moment and a realized victory.

Inspire Hope

Extraordinary leaders offer hope in the midst of intense circumstances. They are aware of how unsettling complexity is to their teams, and they continue to motivate and encourage them through the process. The complexity of leadership is all about seeing through the chaos and casting a compelling vision to lead people through it.

Deciphering complex moments of leadership is not an exact science. It's as easy to get it wrong as it is to get it right, and you're not always going to get it right.

My friend Bill was leading a struggling organization. The staff was making great efforts to turn things around, but it wasn't easy. In fact, Bill would often confide in me his frustrations, fears, and uncertainty about the future. It was an incredibly difficult season, and circumstances were tough.

While Bill didn't make every decision perfectly, what he did exceptionally well was to be honest yet hopeful with his team. When plans didn't work out the way he and his team hoped or a decision he made wasn't the best one, he would acknowledge the problem, correct it, and project a realistic yet optimistic view of the future. Ultimately the organization turned the corner, and it began to realize the success Bill and his team hoped for.

Extraordinary leadership takes courage, intuition, discernment, and prayer. It takes energy, patience, hope, and determination.

Extraordinary leaders step up to help make decisions and to guide the way, especially when circumstances are complex.

Questions for Reflection

- Do you usually avoid tension or embrace it?
- What leadership tension do you need to more purposefully engage right now?
- Is there a way you can take the first step for others?

CHAPTER 3

LEADING FROM WITHIN

Nothing so conclusively proves a man's ability to lead others,
as what he does from day to day to lead himself.[1]

—Thomas J. Watson

I was pretty sure this one was going to be our downfall. It smelled
bad, *really* bad, which was an easy excuse for me to walk away. It
was trashed and disgusting: there were holes in the walls, broken
cabinets, and saturated carpets. But my husband, who buys and
renovates houses for sport, wasn't as quick to give up on this one.
He will purchase a home that has been abandoned and foreclosed
and restore it to a habitable condition.

The transformation of many of these homes is remarkable.
He takes something old and dilapidated and restores it to something of beauty. Most of the time his projects are a great success,
but this is because he has learned the value of looking beyond the
surface appearance to what lies beneath. This one looked hopeless
to me. But my husband wasn't worried about any of the things

that were off-putting to me. I found him scooting through the crawl space under the home, looking for signs of foundational damage. He knows that all the cosmetic interiors are fixable, but if the foundation is compromised, nothing we do for the appearance will matter.

Everything rests on the foundation.

The same is true in our leadership journeys. "Self-leadership" is the foundation. If our foundation is not strong and sturdy, our leadership will never be either. Leadership begins with yourself.

Lead Yourself Well to Lead Others Better

"It's just a busy season. I promise I'll be home more when I finish this project." I apologized to my husband as I raced out the door for any early-morning meeting that would be followed by a full day and a late-night event. When I snuck into bed later that evening hoping I wouldn't wake him, he sighed and quietly said, "It's not just a season, Jen. It's you. There's always another project. There's always more you need to do. It doesn't matter what the job is or who your boss is; you always run yourself ragged. You have to make choices that will sustain you."

As I'm sure you can imagine, I didn't receive his comments well. And it wasn't just that I was tired and irritable; it was because he was right. I knew it, but I didn't want to admit it. I wanted to believe I was the victim of my circumstances, but the truth was that I needed to make some wiser choices and create some healthy boundaries that would enable me to lead better for the long haul. I was touting health and balance to my team but making excuses for why those same principles didn't apply to me.

That discussion and many others like it have caused me to

learn what I believe is one of the most important lessons in leadership: *lead yourself well to lead others better*. It's the grand "aha" of my leadership journey that has become something like beating my head against the proverbial wall. When am I going to get this? When will I understand that I must learn to lead myself well before I ever hope of having a chance to lead and influence others?

Leaders like to lead. And when we say we like to lead, we usually mean we like to lead *others*, right? But if you can't lead yourself well, you will be ill equipped to lead others. This is counterintuitive to our desire to lead. Let's be honest, our desire to lead is often predicated by a desire to control. We may not call it that, but with a little excavation of our hearts, we find our desire to control underlying our motivation.

Part of the responsibility of leadership is understanding our influence on others. Leadership is only as strong as the leader. And that responsibility, if you're grasping the weight of it, is the reason why your leadership journey must begin with leading yourself well. In the book *Type Talk at Work*, a resource that expands upon the Myers-Briggs Type Indicator and explores how the different personality types affect individuals in the work environment, the authors state, "The key to managing others effectively is to manage yourself first. The more you know about yourself, the more you can relate to others from a position of confidence, self-assurance, and strength."[2]

Organizational psychologist and business consultant Mark Freeman defines self-leadership as "the process of influencing ourselves and developing the self-motivation needed to perform."[3] Leading ourselves well is the starting point of leadership because it challenges us to define our motives for leading. It forces us to dig up what lies deep and uncovered. It is the foundation of our leadership.

Tough Truths

I was blessed in the early days of my career to work for some strong, incredibly competent leaders. Not only were they great at leading the organization I was part of, but they took a special interest in developing the primitive leadership instincts they saw in me. They were intentional and purposeful in creating opportunities for me to stretch and grow my leadership muscles. Whether it was giving me a chance to make a presentation at a business meeting or sending me to a conference for continued education, opportunities were extended to me before I knew to ask for them.

That gift of leadership development, however, became my expectation. I thought that I deserved intentional investment like that from my future leaders. Years later I collided with an unmet expectation. I believed that others would always be concerned about my leadership development. I found myself disappointed when other leaders didn't provide growth opportunities for me. That unmet expectation would wake me up to some tough truths that I needed to face if I intended to grow as a leader.

Self-leadership doesn't come without acknowledging some difficult realities. This part of leadership is not glamorous. It doesn't get attention or affirmation. No one is singing your praises for leading yourself well, but I truly believe that if we can get this right, the rest of our leadership becomes an overflow.

Here are a few tough truths that we need to understand about self-leadership:

No one cares more about your personal development than you do.

No one is responsible for your leadership development.

You can't wait for someone else to lead you.

No one owes you leadership.

These truths are tricky. We often don't recognize that we have these expectations because for most of our early lives these are healthy expectations. As we're growing up, we do need someone to care more about our development than we do. We wait for others to lead us, and they are responsible for helping us grow. That's part of the maturing process. Once we grow to adulthood, move into our first apartment, and start having to pay some bills, we're forced to start taking responsibility for ourselves. But when it comes to our personal development, especially in the area of leadership, it's not as easy to know when we've moved from adolescence to adulthood.

In our human development, the real transition to adulthood happens when we begin to take responsibility for ourselves. This explains why some eighteen-year-olds move out, get a job, and make their own way and why too many thirty-year-olds are still squatting in their parents' basement. The same is true for our leadership development. We will never "grow up" in our leadership development until we begin to take responsibility for our growth.

Let's look at these tough truths a little more closely:

No one cares more about your personal development than you do.

No one else is responsible for your leadership development.

The leaders you admire have great intentions. They want to believe in you, support you, and invest in you (at least some of them do). But most of them are doing their best just to take care of themselves. They're so consumed with their own responsibilities and their own development that they have little time or energy left over to look around and see whom they could be helping to develop.

That's not to say that you will never have a leader who sees great potential in you and makes a concerted effort to invest in training you and developing you; this tough truth is more about framing your expectations. If you can take responsibility early for your leadership development, you'll be less likely to flounder around, wasting valuable time wallowing in unmet expectations of the leaders around you.

Your leadership development is your responsibility. Seize it.

Remind yourself every day that you are your best champion. Then when a great leader takes an interest in developing you, it's a bonus and a blessing. Your leadership development is your responsibility. Seize it.

Now, let's turn to the last two truths:

You can't wait for someone else to lead you.
No one owes you leadership.

You're a leader, and that means you've got to lead you. You have to take charge. You have to begin to define where you want to go, what you want to learn, and how you're going to accomplish these things. This doesn't mean, however, that you have to run alone. It just means that you've got to be the kickstarter. Define some next steps, and then pull in some wise counselors for support and guidance.

Leadership development is not a right. It's an opportunity and a privilege. Don't expect it to come to you. Go and get it.

A great example of someone who understood these tough truths was my friend and colleague, Steve. It was almost like the two of us had an unspoken contest over who could learn the most. If our boss talked about a book she was reading, Steve would purchase it and start reading it himself. He was always on the lookout for conferences to attend that would help him develop as a marketing manager. He was intentional about following up with people he met. He was eager to learn from people in both similar and different professions. Steve never wasted an opportunity to learn. He embraced his responsibility for self-leadership, and as a result his career development has never slowed down.

The tough truths of self-leadership aren't meant to frustrate or demotivate you. They're meant to challenge you, because if you understand the hard work of self-leadership and pour yourself into it without expectations of others or an entitled attitude, you will develop the character and core of an extraordinary leader. You will begin to lead yourself well, and from that place you'll be equipped to lead others better.

So just how do we do this?

Heart, Soul, Mind, and Strength

Before we can lead others authentically from our heart, soul, mind, and strength, we need to understand how this framework plays out in our self-leadership.

Heart

Leading from your heart means leading with an understanding of who you are. Your heart is the center of your emotions, desires, and wishes. We must understand what motivates and influences us before we can lead others from a sincere heart. We have the potential to understand others better when we first understand ourselves.

Nature Versus Nurture

Anne deals with tremendous fear of being by herself, especially at night. Every evening when she prepares for bed, she follows a rigorous routine to help alleviate her fears and prepare herself to get a good night's rest. She leashes her seventy-five-pound dog, who is nearly as big as she is, and they walk from room to room checking to make sure every door is locked, every window is shut, every blind is closed, and every closet is clear. If she misses a step in the process, she cannot sleep for fear someone could enter through the place she skipped.

Anne's fear seems a little extreme to most of us, but for her a traumatic one-time experience has affected her behavior for perhaps the rest of her life. It doesn't seem extreme to her. It feels necessary.

Many of us have similar behaviors in areas of our lives, behaviors that affect how we lead and interact with others but perhaps aren't quite as obvious as Anne's late-night safety routine.

Perhaps it was an impossible-to-please parent. Having never quite attained approval, you seek approval and affirmation from every person of authority in your life. Additionally, you may project impossible expectations onto those you lead without even realizing it. Maybe a devastating loss left you in a constant state of fear of loss. This driving fear causes you to lead from an anxious place, never at peace with your circumstances or with other people. If you suffered abuse at some point in your history, you may lead with a very defensive, protective posture that rarely allows others close.

The complexity of God's design of the human psyche fascinates me. We are all different. We've each been shaped not only by the individual wiring that we were born with, but also by the circumstances we've experienced and the people who have influenced us. How we view God, how we interact with others, how we perceive ourselves, how we are influenced by our emotions—all are parts of who we have become. Understanding the impact of all these factors helps us make better sense of ourselves and then ultimately enables us to lead ourselves.

During the early years of my leadership journey, I was unaware of the need for self-leadership. I knew that the circumstances of my life—some good and some bad— had shaped me, but I was unaware of how much they influenced how I was living and leading in the present. While I wouldn't have articulated it this way, to some degree I was operating from an "out of sight, out of mind" mentality.

When I would find myself insecure about a decision, instead of slowing down to understand why I felt insecure, I would just power through, attempting to cover up my feelings of insecurity. Avoidance was my method of choice when it came to my personal growth. I eagerly sought to develop my skills and knowledge as a leader, but I was reluctant to seek development for my emotional and psychological health.

The experiences you have encountered in your life influence you. You can't avoid them. They may trigger fears that challenge you or evoke unmet desires that haunt you. When we understand where our emotional reactions originate, we're better equipped to respond more maturely. A popular personality assessment tool called the Enneagram[4] identifies nine personality traits to which we all align. The tool further defines the desires that motivate us and the fears that most strongly influence our personalities.

Assessments like this can be helpful in our self-leadership because they employ the wisdom of psychologists who have studied human patterns and behaviors and have identified language that can help us better understand what most influences us at a soul level. While tools like this can never fully grasp our unique individuality, they can be a starting point for helping us better understand what may be influencing our behaviors on a subconscious level. Coupled with wise counsel and prayer, a personality assessment can be helpful in naming your core motivation. Understanding our motivations gives us a starting point for growth and change.

Often leaders avoid this type of personal development because this kind of change is gradual and difficult to quantify. We often gravitate instead to new management strategies and formulas because they offer clear steps that we can follow and promise outcomes that are more easily measured. Understanding our personality and motivations is deeper and more difficult work, but it is also where the best of our leadership will emerge.

Introvert Versus Extrovert

There is a common misconception that leaders are extroverts. In reality, leadership depends not on whether you're an introvert or an extrovert, but on whether you understand how your introverted or extroverted nature influences how you lead. Both natures have their strengths, and you will lead better when you understand how to lead from your natural inclination rather than trying to be what you are not.

In her *New York Times* bestselling book, *Quiet: The Power of*

Introverts in a World That Can't Stop Talking, Susan Cain devotes a chapter to "The Myth of Charismatic Leadership," relating stories and historical anecdotes about how culture has led us to presume that more extroverted personalities tend to be better leaders, when in fact the data show that both personalities bring important skills to leadership. One specific example that Cain shares is the belief that talkers are perceived as smarter than quiet types, "even though grade-point averages and SAT and intelligence test scores reveal this perception to be inaccurate." She continues: "The more a person talks, the more other group members direct their attention to him, which means that he becomes increasingly powerful as a meeting goes on."[5] You probably experience this phenomenon too, when a group member with a dominant personality begins to sway a group even if this person's idea is not the best at the table.

It's the understanding of how our extroversion or introversion is perceived by those around us that enables us to learn how to use this part of our personality to our benefit rather than our detriment. In the meeting example above, introverts would do well to be sure their thoughts and ideas make their way into the discussion, while extroverts need to be conscious of how their gregarious, fast-talking nature can allow them to dominate a room and influence decision making.

Independent Versus Interdependent

Another barrier to self-leadership can be an independent nature. Many leaders learn to "go it alone" because their drive for influence necessitates a more aggressive pace than that of their peers. While an element of independence can help you accomplish the dreams and goals you have as a leader, a highly independent attitude can also serve to isolate you. It's important to recognize this and make sure you're availing yourself of the counsel of others. Leadership, by definition, involves working with others. The independent spirit that got you to the leadership seat can also be an avenue to derailment if you are not aware of your tendency to leave others behind.

Soul
Consider Your Character

Character is often defined as who you are when no one is looking. It means purposefully pursuing the elements that will help you grow regardless of whether they get immediate attention. Character is about pursuing Christlikeness. It is experiencing God's best developed in us. In Hebrews, chapter 12, the writer spoke of the importance of God's discipline in our life. Verse 10 says, "God disciplines us for our good, in order that we may share in his holiness." In other words, discipline produces Christlike character. Verse 14 challenges us, "Make every effort to live in peace with everyone and to be holy; without holiness no one will see the Lord." Our greatest motivation as leaders should be our desire for those we lead to see God in us. Without holiness, without godly character, others won't see the Lord.

Our character as leaders is essential for our influence. If people do not see God's work in our lives, we have limited influence by which to lead them. Developing the character of Christ is our ultimate goal. We'll talk more specifically about our spiritual life as leaders in chapter 5.

Developing character produces qualities that cause others to have confidence to follow you as a leader. As you pursue growth in your character, be relentless about defining and developing the qualities that you want to be true of you. What do you want others to say about you when you're not around?

Take Time for Self-reflection

Leaders lead busy lives, and in our haste we can fail to pause. Self-leaders understand the importance of slowing down, and they are disciplined to build in time for self-reflection. They consider their emotions and how these might be influencing their actions. They recognize the pattern of sin in their everyday lives. They slow down to study what is going on in their own hearts. They reflect on how they are balancing their time and commitments. They evaluate how well they are doing in maintaining their priorities.

More than 450 years ago, Saint Ignatius of Loyola developed a model for self-leadership, known as *The Spiritual Exercises*, that would be become the foundation for leadership development for the Jesuits, the religious order he is credited with helping to found. Self-awareness was at the heart of *The Spiritual Exercises*. In the book *Heroic Leadership*, Chris Lowney shared that Ignatius believed "leaders thrive by understanding who they are and what they value, by becoming aware of unhealthy blind spots or weaknesses that can derail them, and by cultivating the habit of continuous self-reflection and learning."[6] His emphasis on self-leadership has been the anchor for a religious order that has not only survived but thrived for nearly five centuries.

Monitor Your Emotional Health

Many leaders begin their leadership journey with the misconception that their emotional life should be compartmentalized from their professional life. In doing so, they ignore warning signs and position themselves for derailment. Pastor Pete Scazzero reports that he was "by all external measures, a successful senior pastor of a large, numerically growing, multi-ethnic church in Queens, New York," when circumstances in his life led him to the realization that he was emotionally unhealthy. He explains, "Entire areas of my life were untouched by the Lord Jesus, by my first seventeen years as a devoted follower of Him, e.g., the ability and permission to feel deeply, the skills to process anger and conflict maturely, the inability to process loss in a way that enlarges the soul, speaking honestly, clearly and respectfully, and the enormous power of our family of origin to impact our present."[7]

There are a number of reasons why we might choose to ignore our emotions. Perhaps your family upbringing taught you to stifle emotions like anger or fear. Maybe you've observed other leaders who believed that leadership involves showing a gruff exterior rather than showing sensitivity or care. Perhaps you were never taught healthy conflict skills.

Whether it's due to our upbringing, our observations of other leaders, or our fear of vulnerability, we as leaders often ignore our emotions. The more responsibility and pressure we feel, the less freedom we perceive that we have to engage the underlying emotions plaguing us. Pastor Scazzero recognized how severely his emotional unhealthiness was affecting his leadership, and that awareness led to a journey that would tremendously change his life.

Our emotional health, or lack thereof, is contagious to others. If we're healthy, we'll encourage health in others. If we're unhealthy, we'll pass on unhealthy habits to others. One team that I worked with was led by a manager who was gruff, impersonal, and impossible to please. Every time the team members showed up for a meeting, they braced themselves for the confrontation. It wasn't uncommon for his frustration to explode in an emotional outburst resulting in either angered reactions or tears. The meetings were typically exhausting and demotivating. What's worse is that even when their manager wasn't present, the team members behaved almost the same way as he did. They had caught his habit of emotional instability and as a result were a highly toxic team.

One critical consequence of leading from emotional unhealthiness is that we operate from a me-centric mentality. We process everything from how it affects us. We become protective and defensive rather than sensitive and aware of others. Our inability to engage our own emotions leaves us completely inept at engaging others. This was true of the manager leading this toxic team. The reality was that he was terrified of personal failure, and his fixation on his own success caused him to be oblivious to how his underlying fear influenced his emotions and in turn his entire team.

Healthy leaders are focused on the needs of others. They don't lose precious time or influence by fretting over their own needs and insecurities. They give generously to those they lead and aren't worried about what they get in return or how accepted they feel. The irony is that the healthy leader ultimately feels the acceptance that every leader actually desires.

Mind

Be a Lifelong Learner

Few things are more inspiring than someone who never stops learning. Sandor Teszler was one of those insatiable minds. A Hungarian Jew who survived the Holocaust, Teszler made his living managing and owning textile mills in Croatia and the United States. While Teszler's ninety-seven years were marked by the spirit of an overcomer, what most inspires me is how he lived out his final years. Teszler spent his retirement auditing more than fifty classes at Wofford College and logging countless hours reading in the library that bears his name.

Teszler embodied the belief that education never ends. Love of learning and a curiosity about life can keep our minds alert and sharp. To keep your mind sharp and to continually expand your thinking, identify the ways you learn best. Understand what environments cause you to grow, and create a rhythm that allows you to foster that growth. One of my great friends, Stephen Brewster, is a creative director and oversees a team of incredibly talented staff and volunteers. Stephen's job is demanding, but he knows that creativity is impossible without exposure to new learning and fresh ideas. Stephen shares two ways that he keeps himself connected to continuous learning:

1. Keep your antenna up all the time. Develop a posture of learning, and remember that inspiration can come from anywhere anytime. Look for ideas in every image you see, every blog or article, every song.
2. Automate inspirational learning. Follow people or brands that inspire you on social media, and subscribe to e-mail lists that send articles that help you stay sharp.

As a leader, you must commit to constant learning and be a fanatic about it.

Read Ferociously

Leaders are readers. The best leaders I know are reading all the time. They recognize the value of expanding their knowledge through reading the wisdom of those who have gone before, and they prioritize time for this discipline.

Since there are so many books to choose from, make it a habit to ask others what they are reading and keep a list of recommendations. When a book has been recommended by two or three different people, it's probably one you should read. Get in the habit of using the spare moments of your day for reading. To maximize your reading opportunities, keep a book with you at all times. I typically have a few books on my phone so that I can read while waiting for an appointment or standing in line. You might also listen to audiobooks on your daily commute. Always be on the lookout for pockets of your routine where you can create disciplined time for reading.

Surround Yourself with People Smarter Than You

If we're not careful, we can easily surround ourselves with people much like ourselves. It's human nature. As they say, "Birds of a feather flock together." So in leadership we can get comfortable spending our time with people who are peers. This is especially compounded by the fact that when you're in a leadership role, you are often one of the more experienced people in the room—that's why you're in the leadership seat.

This dynamic makes it all the more important and all the more challenging for you to find environments where you are not the smartest person at the table. Pastor and author John Ortberg says, "If you're the smartest person in the room, you're in the wrong room."[8] In other words, put yourself in circles where you're going to be positioned to learn. Place yourself in environments that stretch your thinking and challenge your opinions.

Strength
Develop Discipline

"People look at the outward appearance, but the LORD looks at the heart" (1 Samuel 16:7). I normally take great comfort in this scripture because I know that despite the best of intentions, I'm often going to fail. Or at least I'll fail to meet others' expectations of me. I treasure the fact that ultimately God is judging my heart and not my every action. But as leaders, we need to be aware that man looks at the outward appearance. Our actions as leaders speak more loudly than our words. Those we lead and influence will be evaluating our actions, and they will never fully know our hearts. Actions speak louder than intentions. Our leadership will be evaluated by what we do, not what we intend.

I think our on-demand culture has done a disservice to us in recent years. We've created a culture where we can acquire what we want quickly, without a great deal of toil or agony. With a swipe of a piece of plastic, we can take home that new TV or fabulous new dress even though our bank accounts reflect numbers less than zero. We expect to get what we want when we want it. To wait on anything feels like a grotesque failure in customer service. Waiting and working hard are not admirable traits in our impatient society.

How do we develop discipline when discipline by its very nature is countercultural? That's the beauty and the curse. Discipline can be beautiful because it's so radically different from the norm that it stands out. Others notice a well-disciplined person, and while they may not quite understand discipline, they can appreciate it. The results are undeniable.

The curse of discipline is that others aren't going to be singing your praises when you're in the trenches. No one is cheering you on and praising you when the alarm goes off at 4:00 a.m. No one is going to notice and exuberantly praise the reading and studying that you do before the sun comes up. No one is greeting you at the door of the gym with a pep talk and a sports drink. Disciplined moments are lonely moments, but these are the moments that build the foundation of influence.

New York Times bestselling author Tommy Newberry says, "Self-discipline occurs in the moments when intention defeats indulgence, when mission trumps mood, and when spirit conquers sentiment."[9]

To be a disciplined leader, you must adopt several important habits:

Set goals in all areas of life: personal, professional, family, and fun. Goals not set are goals not achieved. Entrepreneur and author Jim Rohn said, "Discipline is the bridge between goals and accomplishment."[10] Disciplined leaders see what they want to accomplish in every facet of life, define the goals to get there, and develop the discipline to get it done. Disciplined leaders organize their lives to reflect what they value most. They are clear about their priorities and are laser focused in accomplishing them.

> **Disciplined moments are lonely moments, but these are the moments that build the foundation of influence.**

Take initiative. Disciplined leaders can be trusted to do what they say they'll do. They are known for getting things done and can be counted on to follow through. Disciplined leaders don't wait to be told to do something. They see a need and fill it.

Know when to say no. Disciplined leaders understand that they are not superhuman. They have come to terms with their limitations and as a result make deliberate choices about what they will or won't do. They know they must play to what is most important, and they are constantly managing the tension of the urgent versus the important. They are hyperaware of the tendency of urgent issues to overtake their lives, and they have the courage to step up and retake control rather than becoming a victim of the tyranny of the urgent.

Be clear on what only you can do. Disciplined leaders understand what they are best at. They know their sweet spot, and they work to play to this strength every single day. They don't get bogged down comparing and competing with others. They focus their time and attention on the roles and tasks that they are best positioned to perform. They know that when everyone plays their respective part to the best of their ability, the whole team is better. They also understand that when they model this belief, it empowers everyone around them to do the same.

Be Self-aware

Most of us have difficulty seeing ourselves as others see us. We can as easily be overimpressed with ourselves as underimpressed. Some of us have overinflated egos, and others of us are so self-deprecating that we suffer from extremely low self-worth. Both ends of the spectrum are dangerous to our ability to lead well. Self-awareness is being observant enough to know when you're getting in the way of yourself. Whether you think too highly of yourself or too little, learning to recognize your tendency in either direction will help you lead from a healthier understanding of who you are. Self-awareness is difficult to measure because we are innately wired for self-deception. It's challenging to admit the areas where we are weak, especially when we know they are areas in which we must grow.

To be a self-aware leader, you must do a few things consistently:

Know your strengths and weaknesses. Know your strengths and own them. The world needs them. But equally know and own your weaknesses. There are just some things that you will never be good at. Be okay with that. Don't try to overcompensate or cover them up. Others see through it. Do attempt to grow, but relieve yourself of the pressure of perfecting the things you are not good at. Kevin Penry, a colleague and remarkable leader, often says, "A sense of inadequacy is the constant companion of self-awareness."[11] To be self-aware, we must keep ourselves tuned into our inadequacies. That awareness allows us to keep a grasp on our reality and our need for other people.

Identify mentors and continuously seek counsel. You will never outgrow the need for wisdom. From whom do you receive regular feedback? Mentors can come in many shapes and forms. Some mentors in my life are peers who I admire for certain strengths. By getting to know them better, I learn more about how they have developed their strengths. Others are more experienced experts in my field of work. Often it's difficult to identify mentors who can commit to ongoing relationships, so I will request a lunch or coffee meeting. In that meeting I seek to glean as much wisdom as I can. If our meeting develops into an ongoing relationship, that's great, but either way I have learned more than I would have if I had not met with this person at all.

Look for voices in your life that provide consistent and honest input. Who speaks to your spiritual growth, your family life, your character, and your performance? Find these voices and seek them out regularly.

Always evaluate what you need to "own" (good or bad) in every situation. Whatever the circumstance that you find yourself in, you played a part in the outcome. What do you need to learn from it? What did you do well? What could you have done better? How did you influence others? Reflecting on key conversations, decisions, actions, and outcomes can provide great clarity about how to navigate future situations.

Self-leadership is the hard work behind the scenes that prepares you for great leadership. Cultivating your character, developing discipline, and seeking greater self-awareness provide the framework for developing the leadership of self.

Getting Uncomfortable

Self-leadership is a willingness to make yourself uncomfortable in order to lead yourself and others to bigger dreams and greater goals. It requires the humility of introspection. Humility may make us uncomfortable, but if endured it produces results that are often scarce. Seth Godin explains it this way:

> Leadership is scarce because few people are willing to go through the discomfort required to lead. This scarcity makes leadership valuable. . . . It's uncomfortable to stand up in front of strangers. It's uncomfortable to propose an idea that might fail. It's uncomfortable to challenge the status quo. It's uncomfortable to resist the urge to settle. When you identify

the discomfort, you've found the place where a leader is needed. If you're not uncomfortable in your work as a leader, it's almost certain you're not reaching your potential as a leader.[12]

This is exactly why leadership is necessary, and it's also why extraordinary leaders are unusual. Many leaders skip over self-leadership because the discomfort of facing their own limitations is frightening enough to discourage them before they've even begun.

Getting Honest

As we begin to dive into each of the four dimensions, consider the following list of behaviors and situations that might indicate a disproportionate balance of the dimensions in your leadership. See if one dimension of leadership resonates with you more than the others. How do the items that apply to you on this list compare to the results of your assessment (see page 11)?

You might be a disproportionately heart-full (relational) leader if

- Your door is always open. No interruption is a bad interruption.
- You keep poorly performing employees much longer than you should.
- All your employees think they are your best friend.
- You have trouble giving constructive feedback to anyone.
- You react emotionally to challenges and problems.
- Meetings you lead are notorious for a lot of talk but little action.

- Your staff members feel well loved but don't know what they should be doing.

You might be a disproportionally soul-full (spiritual) leader if

- You end every conversation with "I'm praying for you," but you don't actually do it.
- Your language is laced with Christian platitudes like "God will make a way" or "God is in control."
- Your spiritual practices feel routine rather than genuine.
- You are known for speaking boldly about your faith yet are equally known for being insensitive and uncaring. In other words, you talk the talk but don't walk the walk.

You might be a disproportionately mind-full (managerial) leader if

- You are all business all the time.
- Your schedule is packed from morning to night.
- You are impatient with the progress of the team.
- You are always striving to improve yourself, the organization, and the team.
- Your staff members feel like they know very little about you or other team members.
- Your staff members complain about feeling overworked even though they are not putting in late nights.

You might be a disproportionately strength-full (visionary) leader if

- You have more ideas than you have time to implement.
- Others roll their eyes when you have a new idea.
- Your team members feel like you leave them in the dust. While they are dealing with the reality of implementation, you are off dreaming up new possibilities. They don't trust that you understand what it takes to make your ideas come to fruition.
- You are more respected outside your organization than inside your organization.

None of us are naturally great at all the dimensions. Leading with our whole selves is a process that we must commit to if we're serious about being extraordinary leaders. When you grow as a leader, your organization will grow and the people you lead will grow. In their book *Spiritual Leadership*, Henry and Richard Blackaby explain, "The greatness of an organization is directly proportional to the greatness of its leader. . . . As leaders grow personally, they increase their capability to lead. As they increase their capability to lead, they enlarge the capacity of their organization to grow."[13]

When we lead ourselves well, we are equipped to lead others better. In developing our character, we become more consistent and dependable. As we are more aware of the discipline we need, our focus and productivity increases. When our self-awareness grows, we become aware of how our personality affects our leadership. As we are more aware of our emotional health, we experience greater balance and peace of mind.

The great irony of self-leadership is that as we grow more effective at leading ourselves, we become more selfless. Healthy self-leadership provides the perspective from which we become *more* other-centric rather than self-centered. By tackling some of the challenges that tend to derail or distract us, we become better equipped to focus on developing a healthy balance of the dimensions of extraordinary leadership.

Questions for Reflection

- What unhealthy expectations have you had of the leaders around you?
- How does your personality affect your leadership?
- Which disciplines do you need to develop to grow in your self-leadership?

PART 2

THE DIMENSIONS OF EXTRAORDINARY

I am here to seduce you into a love of life; to help you to become a little more poetic; to help you die to the mundane and to the ordinary so that the extraordinary explodes in your life.[1]

—Bhagwan Shree Rajneesh

CHAPTER 4

LEAD WITH ALL YOUR HEART

Trust men and they will be true to you: treat them
greatly and they will show themselves great.[1]

—Ralph Waldo Emerson

It was August 1978 and the crowds were thick in St. Peter's Square, expectant and hopeful for the inauguration of their new pope, John Paul I. But in a startling turn of events, the same crowds found their way back to St. Peter's a mere six weeks later due to the sudden death of their newly appointed pontiff.

Amid confusion, mourning, and skepticism, Pope John Paul II accepted the papal responsibility. To make matters worse for the locals, he was the first non-Italian pope since the Dutchman, Adrian VI, who was elected in 1522. Pope John Paul II's appointment wasn't expected. He wasn't anticipated. If anything, the church was skeptical, and the world was watching.

But Pope John Paul II did something unprecedented for the papacy: he addressed the crowd directly. He smiled. He spoke in the crowd's native tongue of Italian, one of twelve languages in which he was fluent. He acknowledged the potential mistakes he might make with the spectators' language and invited them to correct him when he did. Eric Metaxas, author of *7 Men and the Secret of Their Greatness*, describes the scene: "His openness, vulnerability, and humor drew laughter and applause from the crowd. By the time the extemporaneous speech drew to a close, a remarkable thing had happened: the crowd that was surprised and confused before was now wholeheartedly on John Paul II's side."[2]

When John Paul II stepped up that day to assume his new responsibility of leadership, he became real. He became relatable. He displayed how an extraordinary leader comprehends and employs the relational dimension of leadership. He led from his heart. Metaxas explains, "Part of the greatness of this man was his extraordinary ability to communicate humbly and humorously and clearly. There can be no other word for it: he was charming. Like a great politician but without a hint of guile, he managed to connect with his audiences in a way that delighted them."[3]

Leading from the heart means understanding the power of connection: knowing that one of our greatest human needs is to be known. John Ortberg expresses it this way: "The yearning to attach and connect, to love and be loved, is the fiercest longing of the soul."[4] We want to believe that we matter. And we sincerely long for those who lead us to see us as individuals: to see our unique potential and contribution, to help call it out in us, and to affirm that what we bring and who we are really matter to the greater story.

When we lead from the heart, we earn influence with others

through relationship rather than authority. Relational leaders realize that title and position only get you so far, but the places you can take a team with relational influence are endless. Relational leaders understand that people follow leaders not for the leader but for themselves.

People follow leaders who inspire them to believe greater things about themselves. In his immensely popular TED Talk titled "How Great Leaders Inspire Action," Simon Sinek says, "People don't buy what you do. They buy why you do it." He continues, "What you do simply proves what you believe."[5] If what you do communicates what you believe, what are your actions saying about what you believe about those you lead? When we relationally connect with those we lead, we communicate value and worth.

Leading Like a "Lovecat"

For my friend Kat, leading from the heart is as natural as breathing. Relational leadership is so instinctual to her that she can't imagine leading any other way. Kat and I became friends when we were starting out in our careers. Bright, wide-eyed, eager twenty-somethings, we both attacked our first job opportunity with an attempt to prove to the world that we had what it takes to succeed.

While we had incredible drive and passion to prove ourselves, we were motivated in different ways. I was inclined to believe that hard work, diligent effort, thorough reports, and great achievements would get me noticed. Kat, on the other hand, believed that intentional relationships, genuine care, and networking would be her path to success.

We both were partially correct. While my more managerial style of leadership was important, I initially missed the value of the relational dimension of leadership in which Kat was naturally adept. In fact, I would often get annoyed that Kat seemed to always have a "people first" mentality, especially when there were so many tasks we needed to accomplish. This tension became particularly hairy when we were partnered up for a project. We repeatedly approached the task from completely different viewpoints.

On one of our business trips, the meeting with a client had gone long and we needed to leave as soon as possible to catch our flight. As the meeting wrapped up, I gathered our things and was hurrying out the door only to discover that Kat wasn't with me. Thinking she had perhaps stopped to go to the restroom, I impatiently waited for a few minutes. When it seemed a reasonable amount of time had passed, I went to look for her. To my dismay, she was still back in the conference room talking with our client. Giving her the evil eye to express our need to get moving didn't seem to speed her up. She finished the conversation, shook hands, gave hugs, and swapped phone numbers like they were best friends. The client loved her. He hardly noticed me. As I peeled out of the parking lot, anxious to get us to the airport, she exuberantly shared that the client had committed to our project. Those last five minutes she spent with him had sealed the deal.

I was both excited and irritated. Kat's awareness of the need to spend those extra few relational minutes had led us to the result we hoped for. While I was stressing out over a potential missed flight, she was more concerned about taking care of the client.

I'm often amazed that our friendship withstood the tension of those early days. Young and ambitious, we both were inclined to believe that our own way was best. Over time we began to value each other's approach. I soon recognized that thinking about others first was the best way to start a project. We will rarely get the opportunity to lead managerially if we haven't first connected with the hearts of people. Kat also discovered the place for my strategic, no-nonsense, dig-deep-and-map-out-a-plan, action orientation. Eventually we had to put feet to everything we dreamed about. We got it. We got each other, and I dare say we're both better for it.

While leading relationally was easy for Kat, it was much more difficult for me. Committed to growing and learning together, we often studied different management and leadership books. One season we were a part of a larger group that read Tim Sanders's book *Love Is the Killer App*. This book blew my mind! Sanders strongly argues for the value of love in our working relationships. He coins the term "lovecat" (which frankly still makes me uncomfortable) to describe people who employ the ingredients that he believes differentiate great leaders:

1. Knowledge: offering your wisdom freely
2. Network: giving your address book to everyone who wants it
3. Compassion: always being human[6]

Sanders believes, "Those of us who use love as a point of differentiation in business will separate ourselves from our competitors just as world-class distance runners separate themselves from the rest of the pack trailing behind them."[7]

As uncomfortable as Sanders's lovecat theory made me, I believed it because I had seen it in action in the life of my friend

Kat. Kat was the consummate lovecat, and I had a lot to learn from her.

Emotional Intelligence

Our heart is the seat of our emotions. It's where we feel the deepest. Love, joy, fear, sorrow, jealousy, hatred—if you feel it, you feel it from your heart. Most of us fall in one of two camps: we either embrace our emotions and are comfortable with being considered "emotional," or we resist emotions and attempt to remain unemotional.

In one particularly difficult season of my life, I resolved to never cry again. I had dealt with a series of losses, and I was tired of feeling the grief. I put an emotional wall up that day that became a troublesome barrier in my relationships for many years to come. I found great pride in not showing emotion. The truth was that I was still feeling emotions, but I was creating unhealthy ways to process them. My stoicism not only hindered me from dealing with grief, loss, and fear, but also robbed me of enjoying love, peace, and joy.

God created us in his image, and emotions are a part of that package. Feeling emotion isn't the problem. Our response to those emotions is what either helps or hinders us. As leaders, we need to understand how our emotions affect us.

In recent years considerably more time and attention is being devoted to the conversation of emotional intelligence in the workplace. Emotional intelligence, or EQ as it is commonly referred to, is defined by MHS, a company that administers EQ assessments, as "a set of emotional and social skills that influence the way we perceive and express ourselves, develop and maintain social relationships, cope with challenges, and use emotional informa-tion in an effective and meaningful way."[8] Essentially it's about understanding how our emotions influence our work life.

Daniel Goleman, author of the book *Working with Emotional Intelligence*, observes, "More and more companies are seeing that encouraging emotional intelligence skills is a vital component of any organization's management philosophy."[9] He continues, "Businesses are waking up to the fact that even the most expen-sive training can go awry, and often does. And this ineptness comes at a time when emotional intelligence in individuals and organizations is emerging as a missing ingredient in the recipe for competitiveness."[10]

To a good degree the emotional intelligence conversation really straddles the heart and soul of leadership development. Our EQ includes our ability to understand how our emotions affect us as well our ability to read the emotions of others and discern how we're affecting others. EQ enables us to determine the emotional dynamics with others and navigate relationships in effective ways.

A common example of someone who lacks emotional intelli-gence in the workplace is the boss everyone fears. Motivated by stress and the pressure that sits on his shoulders, an emotionally inept leader responds curtly to staff questions, explodes when deadlines are missed, and conveys frustration when interrupted even for legitimate questions. His lack of engagement communi-cates annoyance and impatience.

What this leader fails to recognize are the underlying emo-tions that are causing him to be curt, to explode, to convey frustration, or to be aloof. What is the fear or pressure that is draw-ing out these behaviors? If he is unwilling to face these emotions, he will never be in a position to better handle them. Additionally, he is clueless as to how his emotions are affecting the emotions of his team. His staff members are likely to avoid engaging with him for fear of all the responses described. They will attempt to solve problems on their own or with one another but may often miss out on the wisdom the leader could bring, therefore making additional mistakes or causing problems for the organization.

These unhealthy emotional habits create a cycle that perpetuates additional emotional dysfunction in the organization. The leader lashes out, the employees retreat, the leader lashes out again because of problems created by the employees' retreat, and the employees put up further emotional defenses and keep an even greater distance. No one wins and the organization suffers.

As leaders, we have the responsibility and the power to break this cycle, but to do this, we must first develop greater emotional intelligence. Everything rises or falls on leadership, so we must lead ourselves well in this area in order to lead others too. I believe that emotional intelligence will continue to be a key differentiating factor for extraordinary leaders.

Encouragement

Leaders must be encouragers. Remember that we as leaders must be dealers in hope. We must keep hope and possibility in front of those we lead, and every person needs to be given the hope and possibility for personal success. As a leader, you need to be aware that your feedback carries substantial weight. Because you sit in a seat of authority, what you say matters and has a distinct impact on those you lead.

But for encouragement to be effective, it must be balanced with candor. Praise is only meaningful when it's given by someone who will also compel you to grow. Encouragement is a two-sided coin. Leaders who encourage well are skilled at praising the positive and coaching for improvement. To encourage, as defined by *Merriam-Webster*, is "to inspire with courage, spirit, or hope; to spur on; to give help; to foster."[11] This reinforces the thought that encouragement is not simply happy talk. Encouragement is an intentional action by the leader to provide feedback that seeks to develop the best in others. Relational leaders take ownership for the development of those they lead and seek opportunities to speak into them in every interaction.

I once had a leader who was always very kind but wasn't actually very encouraging. It wasn't uncommon for her to say "Good job" after I made a presentation or led a meeting, but she rarely said more than that. "Good job" was never followed with what was good about my performance or what could have been even better. The only indicator I usually had that I was underperforming was her silence. I had worked with this leader long enough to understand this about her and found other people who could provide the encouragement I needed to help me develop, but I believe that there was always a gap in our relationship because of her limited ability to provide encouraging feedback. Our working relationship, although very significant, always felt quite shallow when it came to the relational dimension of leadership.

Although my manager wasn't extremely critical, her lack of encouragement caused me to be hesitant. When leaders understand the importance of providing encouragement, they communicate that they value those they lead. The healthy balance of praise and feedback that constitutes encouragement reflects a leader's esteem for the receiver. When employees feel valued, you will get the best out of them.

Connection

I grew up accustomed to the idea of hierarchy. The manufacturing companies that dominate the Midwest have influenced the culture with their very systematic, some would say bureaucratic, approach to management and leadership. In my experience that approach carried over to most arenas of life. If someone was in charge, whether he or she was a teacher in the classroom, a parent in the home, a pastor in the church, or a boss in the workplace, it was your responsibility to listen. It didn't matter if this person was effective, engaging, or even kind. The order of things demanded engagement regardless of whether you were inspired by and connecting with the leader.

I often found myself annoyed with people who were disrespectful of whoever was speaking. Being the model pupil that I was, I just figured other students were not as serious about their studies. If people walked out during the message at church on Sunday to use the restroom, I judged them as not being committed to their faith. I made all kinds of assumptions about people, often judging their actions. It never occurred to me that perhaps their disengagement could have more to do with the communicator.

Naively, I expected the same level of engagement from others that I gave to them. As my career path developed and I earned more and more opportunities to communicate publicly, I found myself incredibly frustrated by people's lack of focus. I remember that on one particular Sunday morning when I was communicating announcements in the worship service, the couple in the front row were whispering to each other, a mom was shushing her kids, another two ladies walked out of the room, and another guy was asleep. Was anyone listening to a word that I was sharing?

Consumed with all the distractions, I was certain that what I had to share didn't have a chance of being compelling. Let's be honest: I was delivering the announcements. I already had several strikes against me. I was unloading information rather than providing inspiration.

Connecting is one of the most important tasks of leadership. In order to lead others to new ideas, to goals, and to action, we must first be able to connect with them. We must demand their attention, but not in a dictatorial way. We must do it in a way that connects with their hearts and compels them to listen. We must seek to relate to them, which in turn increases our influence.

Connecting as a relational leader takes us back to the pivotal understanding of leadership: leadership is about others. It's not about you. In order to connect, we must see those we're leading as the center of our attention and conversation. The only chance we have of getting our purpose accomplished is to make our purpose secondary to the needs of those we're leading. We must understand whom we're leading and connect with them before we can ever hope to influence them with our agenda.

Gregarious, Charming, or Just Ordinary

There is a prevalent misconception that great leaders are gregarious and charming. We assume that leaders must have the ability to motivate an audience like Martin Luther King Jr., the ability to charm and delight viewers like Audrey Hepburn, and the ability to command an arena like U2 or Garth Brooks. We have all seen these people and have probably wanted to channel their allure at some point in our leadership journey. And while gregarious and charming is great, not all of us are wired for that, nor do we need to be. Leadership looks different on each of us, and it looks extraordinary when it looks like us.

We earn our best relational leadership influence when we have a healthy understanding of ourselves. Some leaders are best in groups, others are great one-on-one, and still others are great through writing. Where does your personality shine? Learn this about yourself, and then adapt to make the best use of it.

If you connect best with others via writing, make a habit of sending personal notes to your staff each week. If your heart is most understood when you sit face-to-face with others, plan meetings that allow for in-person interaction on a regular basis. If you are energized by facing a full room and rallying the energy of the masses, create a rhythm for regular staff meetings that allows you to do this frequently. If you communicate well through video, send a video message or schedule video chats.

Customize the ideas to play to your relational strengths. If you question where you're relationally the strongest, ask the people closest to you, such as family members, and they will provide you with valuable insights on how you best connect with others.

Build Rapport

Great leaders build rapport with their team. They communicate whether in word or in action their desire to build a relationship with their staff. Some theories of management suggest that professional and personal lines should not be crossed, and while there are appropriate lines that need to be considered, I believe there are healthy ways to build friendships with those you lead.

A leader at a large nonprofit begins every working relationship with new executive team members by telling them, "I want to be the world's leading expert on who you are and how you're doing." This profound expression communicates to his staff members that he wants to know them not just for what they contribute to the organization, but for what makes them thrive, what inspires them, and what motivates them. He speaks to their hearts by communicating that who they are matters. He values their need to be known.

Earn Influence

Extraordinary leaders recognize that every relational connection with those they lead has the potential to increase their influence.

Influence is earned over time with consistent engagement and faithful action. Leadership coach and consultant Dan Rockwell observes, "People are influenced by those who understand them. Permission to lead is given by those who feel known, appreciated, affirmed, and respected. When people feel you understand their talents, drives, hopes, and fears you earn their consent to lead."[12]

> **Extraordinary leaders recognize that every relational connection with those they lead has the potential to increase their influence.**

Think about the people who have influence with you. Chances are they are people who have been consistently and faithfully involved in your life. They are concerned about more than just your performance. You know they genuinely care about you.

Build Trust

In Stephen M. R. Covey's *New York Times* bestseller, *The Speed of Trust*, Covey asserts that trust is the one thing that changes everything.

He claims that it is the "one thing which, if removed, will destroy the most powerful government, the most successful business, the most thriving economy, the most influential leadership, the greatest friendship, the strongest character, the deepest love. On the other hand, if developed and leveraged, that one thing (trust) has the potential to create unparalleled success and prosperity in every dimension of life."[13]

Trust feels like a very arbitrary thing to build. How do you know when you've earned it? Who defines it, you or the other party? And as arbitrary as it may be, we quickly know when we don't have it.

Jake was the newly appointed leader of a nonprofit. He came in on the heels of a well-loved retiring predecessor. While there was little debate among the board members about appointing Jake, it was clear right from the start that it was going to take time for him to earn the trust of this team. The team's years of familiarity with the former leader had left Jake with an uphill battle. To make matters worse, there was a lot of work to be done. The organization was in an operational shamble. While the team had loved the previous leader, it had tended to overlook the lack of organizational leadership that had resulted in revenue decline and disengagement from donors. The issues that seemed obvious to Jake were highly sensitive to others. Jake had a long road of trust building ahead of him.

Jake quickly learned what Stephen M. R. Covey explains in his book: "Trust is a function of two things: character and competence. Character includes your integrity, your motive, and your intent with people. Competence includes your capabilities, your skills, your results, and your track record. And both are vital."[14] While it was not an easy or speedy process, Jake earned trust with the organization by displaying great character and competence. Jake was dependable. He followed through on commitments. He was careful to explain the heart behind controversial decisions.

While people didn't always agree with every decision Jake made, they trusted his motives because he took the time to explain them. Over time favorable results and the successful launch of new initiatives added to Jake's credibility. People began to trust that he would do what he said he would do. His commitment to building trust earned Jake the influence to lead the organization back to health and to ultimately achieve the goals it aspired to.

Create a Healthy Environment

Leaders are keepers of culture. They know that great team cultures require deliberate effort. Teams will work better with one another, they'll go above and beyond the call of duty, they'll invest themselves personally, and they'll own their wins and their losses more honestly when they are a part of a healthy environment. Healthy environments are of course characterized by leaders of integrity; intolerance for discrimination; strong systems, policies, and procedures; and an organizational alignment that promotes shared goals and achievable results.

But truly healthy cultures go one step further. The healthiest work cultures I've observed find ways to capture the spirit of the organization. They have identified the "personality" of the organization, and they find ways to express that. Personality provides color and vibrancy to what could otherwise be a strong but sterile environment.

Ranked number 1 in *Fortune* magazine's 2014 list of the 100 Best Companies to Work For, Google is well known for its corporate culture.[15] When I moved to the Silicon Valley area, one of the first places I visited was the Google campus. I had heard rumors of the great megaplex in Mountain View, California, and my quick tour lived up to the hype. Reflecting a desire to keep the culture of a start-up organization, everything about the Google campus is designed to inspire open communication among employees. From bicycles to bowling alleys to inspiring themed meeting spaces, the facilities encourage interaction in fun and innovative ways.

Zappos, an online retailer that aims to "deliver WOW through service," carries that wow factor into the culture for its staff. The managers refer to their staff as family and have ten core family values that they believe put the "zap" in Zappos. Among them you'll see phrases like "create fun and a little weirdness" and "be adventurous, creative, and open-minded."[16]

Several years ago I toured the Zappos offices. On our tour the other visitors and I were made kings and queens for a day, complete with throne and regalia; challenged to a hula-hoop contest; given a free book from the company's family library; and paraded through a sea of cubicles where staff, or "family members," were bustling with energy and productivity. The energy in the space made me briefly consider a career change.

> **Great team cultures should cause people to clamor to work for your team.**

In their book *Spiritual Leadership*, Henry and Richard Blackaby state, "Today's workplace is a forum for people to express themselves and to invest their efforts into something that contributes positively to society. People no longer choose jobs based merely on salary and benefits. They seek companies with corporate values that match their personal values."[17] Great team cultures should cause people to clamor to work for your team, your division, or your company. People aren't afraid to work. They're afraid to have to work in a place that drains the life out of them.

Love Your Team

Love your team. Channel your inner lovecat. It's essential. As leaders, we are entrusted with the amazing responsibility of stewarding the gifts and talents of our staff. Our greatest joys can be found in doing what business consultant and writer Jim Collins taught us: placing the right people in the right seats doing the right things. There's a magic that happens when an entire team is flourishing.

In his leadership podcast, Andy Stanley, lead pastor of North Point Ministries, talked about a series of Sundays when instead of preaching, he went around to all the ministry's Atlanta-area campuses and observed the teams in action. He came away from that experience incredibly proud of his teams and the work they were doing. In fact, he was so proud of his teams that he spent time with their leaders making sure they all understood what was working and why. Instead of resting on his laurels, he dug deeper to understand why what his team leaders were doing was working, so that they would be equipped to continue their success.

Every employee deserves to know that they are a vital part of the team. They need to understand how his or her gifts contribute to the organization. We must seek ways to remind them of the significance of their work. Every role is important. Every task is essential. Every person who fulfills a role or performs a task is vital to living out the mission of the organization. When you connect the dots for people and affirm their strengths and contributions, you inspire self-worth that feeds their souls.

Build a Stronger Team

For all the reasons we've been discussing, leading from the heart builds stronger teams. People are more committed when they feel cared for.

Living in Silicon Valley has allowed me the opportunity to connect with some brilliant minds. As I sit here typing on my MacBook Air, reading books on my iPad, and listening to music on my iPhone, I'm reminded of my first conversation with Ron Johnson, the former VP of retail for Apple.

Johnson was responsible for the launch of the Apple retail stores. When I asked him what made the stores successful, I was taken aback a bit by his first response. Instead of discussing marketing strategy and business plans, Johnson lit up with energy about the importance of the team. He summarized for me what he's said in a number of interviews: "The most important component to the Apple experience is that the staff isn't focused on selling stuff. It's focused on building relationships and trying to make people's lives better."[18] Johnson believes that relationships unlock engagement. When we can connect with people, we learn what matters to them, and we're more able to help them accomplish their goals or meet their needs.

Johnson's leadership at Apple demonstrated his understanding of the power of relational leadership. From hiring to training to coaching, Johnson relationally connected with his team and inspired them to do the same with one another and with their customers. The result was a new division of business for Apple that not only revolutionized how computers are sold but established a new standard for customer service.

Show Compassion

Recognized for pioneering the field of modern nursing, Florence Nightingale had to fight to find fulfillment for her compassionate spirit in this calling. Although facing strong opposition from her family for not following the traditional path of wife and mother that was expected of an affluent young Englishwoman, Nightingale was moved by her belief that God had called her to her vocation. She wrote, "God called me in the morning and asked me would I do good for him alone without reputation."[19]

Relational leaders demonstrate compassion. Compassionate leaders are more concerned about providing care than taking credit. When compassion drives us, it makes way for humility to lead us. In Florence Nightingale's case, her passion was for providing better patient care. Troubled by the insufficient care and horrible conditions provided to wounded soldiers, Nightingale committed her life to improving care and reducing suffering for patients. Additionally, she funded a hospital and training school for nurses as well as programs for improved sanitation in India. Her compassion led her to focus on a problem that she devoted her life to solving.

Often the demands of leadership can disconnect us from what first inspired us to pursue the ministries or careers in which we are leaders. We must find ways to stay connected to that heart of compassion from which we started. Personally, I have great compassion for young, developing leaders. One of my greatest joys is seeing young people given opportunities to exercise their primitive leadership muscles. Wherever I am on the organizational chart, I'm always looking for ways to invite young leaders into conversations. Staying connected to them keeps me connected to my raw leadership passion.

When Your Heart Gets in the Way

Don had no trouble leading from his heart. In fact, often Don's heart got in the way of his leadership. It wasn't noticeable at first. Don's caring spirit and gentle demeanor quickly won him influence with his colleagues. He was helpful and truly enjoyed taking time to talk other employees through the complexities of the operational issues that he oversaw.

The dark side of Don's relational leadership style was that his emotions often got the best of him. The very part of his personality that enabled him to connect well with others also caused him to obsess over being liked, respected, and included. Don's emotional neediness eventually put a lid on his leadership. His constant need for affirmation and inclusion became exhausting to those who led him. Additionally, Don implemented some systems with his team that, while appearing helpful in the short run, created habits that were unsustainable in the long run. His good, heartfelt intentions actually created more frustration for his coworkers. He made decisions that made him a hero in the present but created dysfunctions for the future.

If Don had engaged more of his mind to think through his strategies and had used more of his visionary strength to consider the future, he would have been less reactive to his heart leadership, which when left to operate independently led to shortsighted, emotionally charged decisions.

It's not uncommon for our heart to get in the way from time to time. Your emotional needs can get unbalanced, and you can unintentionally become needy and dependent on others for your sense of value or worth. There are also other ways your heart may get in the way:

Being a friend when you need to be an authority. I'm a firm believer that friendship can exist within the workplace. I've been extraordinarily fortunate to have some of my greatest friendships emerge from working relationships. However, when we're in a position of leadership, there will be moments when we need to make a tough decision or provide constructive feedback.

When you lead from the heart, it's easy to get soft on others in regard to expectations. Leading from the heart doesn't mean we abandon accountability. In fact, when we love others well, we should be even more inclined to love them enough to make them better. Our job as leaders is not to make people happy. It's to make people better.

Being fake when you need to be authentic. Particularly for those of us with more outgoing or charismatic personalities, we must avoid letting our relational leadership become forced or manipulative. When we realize that leading with the heart engages others, we can be tempted to manufacture emotion to generate the response we want. Our relational leadership can then quickly become forced and inauthentic.

The popular Clifton StrengthsFinder[20] assessment contrasts the WOO (Winning Others Over) theme with the Relator theme. Those with the strength of WOO are quick to make connections, but those connections may be at risk of remaining shallow. In contrast, those with the Relator theme enjoy building deep, lasting relationships. It's not that one or the other is better. We simply need to understand how we naturally connect with others and seek to be authentic in our relational leadership.

Leading with Heart

Stoic. Stone cold. Heartless. We've all experienced leaders who seem to lack any ounce of emotion. Some environments, especially for marketplace leaders, encourage us to leave our hearts at home when we go to work. In an attempt to be professional and respected, we close off our hearts from engaging with those around us. We don't want to be perceived as soft or emotional, so we wall off our hearts.

But leading without engaging our hearts leaves our leadership cold and lifeless. We inadvertently leave the people around us feeling nonhuman or guilty for having emotions of their own. When we aren't our authentic selves, we don't give others permission to be their authentic selves either.

Leading from our hearts doesn't come without intentionality. There are choices that we need to make every day to help us create relational leadership habits. Here are some techniques to consider:

Slow down to see people. Leaders are often in positions of influence because they get stuff done. They have proven their competency and have been rewarded with greater responsibility. This means we're often driven by task and the agenda that awaits us each day. In order to lead from the heart, we have to slow down to see people.

One way that I try to do this is to play what I call the "Make Somebody's Day" game. I've determined to approach each day with the intention of finding someone to give an extra blessing to. It might mean paying for someone's meal, leaving a generous tip for waitstaff, giving someone a genuine compliment, or performing some other gesture of kindness. The point is to identify an opportunity and seize it.

Build time for conversation. Leaders lead hurried lives. Driven by the clock and our commitments, we can turn every interaction into a hurried string of instructions. Whether it's with your family, friends, or staff, make sure that your communication with them doesn't only revolve around what you need from them. Do you know what your child's greatest fear is? Have you asked your spouse what he or she is worried about? Do you know what personal pressure is stressing out your staff member? The people around you are not going to feel comfortable sharing what is weighing on their hearts if your anxious nature is dominating the conversation. Be sure you're building in time for genuine interaction with those you lead. Arrange your schedule to leave time for conversations to breathe. Real connection happens when we slow down.

One of the ways I do this is by devoting an hour a week to each person I directly manage. This can create great demands on my schedule, but by scheduling weekly time with each person, I know that I'll have the opportunity to check in about more than just the impending deadline we're working on. I usually plan for the first part of our meeting to be time to catch up. This is the time for me to ask people about their families and how they are doing personally. These one-on-one meetings are some of my most valuable leadership conversations every week.

Have fun with your team. Let your team know you're human. Don't take yourself too seriously. Make room for laughter and celebration. Remember, your staff takes its cues from you. If you don't make fun a part of your culture, no one else will. Cater lunch in celebration of a team victory. Celebrate birthdays with cake and ice cream. Determine what works for your culture, and commit to creating memorable, fun, enjoyable moments.

Show appreciation. Everyone wants to be recognized for who they are. Bestselling author and motivational speaker Tommy Newberry says, "If you want to increase the value of something in your life, take better care of it. If you want to increase the value of key relationships, treasure them. . . . Honor them with more interest and attention. Dwell on what's good about them—there is always something that's great or could be great."[21] The temptation in leadership is to focus on what's not working rather than what is. Fight this temptation daily. Be on the lookout for people who are doing well, and go out of your way to acknowledge their achievements. Appreciation and affirmation are enormous trust builders. All team members want to know they matter. It's your job as a leader to ensure that they know their work is valued.

The heart of leadership is the start of leadership. When we connect with the heart, we earn influence to lead with soul, mind, and strength. Consider your relational leadership influence: How are you connecting with those you lead? Do they know you're for them and that you value them? Do they know how their work affects the entire team? Do you know their stories and what inspires them and motivates them? Every relational connection you make gives you greater opportunity to lead.

Questions for Reflection

- What is one way that you could encourage or connect with your staff this week?
- How could you make your workplace culture more fun and engaging?
- To whom do you need to show more compassion?

CHAPTER 5

LEAD WITH ALL YOUR SOUL

The choice to lead from our soul is a vulnerable approach to leadership, because the soul is more tender than the mind or the ego.[1]

—Ruth Haley Barton

Dietrich Bonhoeffer is widely recognized for being a Christ-follower who was willing to remain true to his faith whatever the cost. A pastor, theologian, writer, and speaker, Bonhoeffer is most remembered for his staunch resistance to Nazi dictatorship, which led to his arrest, imprisonment in a concentration camp, and tragic execution. In his brief thirty-nine years of life, Bonhoeffer left a legacy that clearly evidenced where his ultimate faith and loyalty lay. In the book *7 Men and the Secret of Their Greatness*, Eric Metaxas says this: "Bonhoeffer explained that true authority must, by definition, be submitted to a higher authority—which is to say, God—and true leadership must be servant leadership."[2]

Dietrich Bonhoeffer understood at an extreme level what it looks like for our faith to lead first. There can be little question that leading from his soul was a guiding principle in his life. His faith informed his decisions even when those decisions were in such tremendous opposition to the culture of the day. According to Eberhard Bethge, his student and biographer, with war imminent and Hitler's army building, Bonhoeffer made a trip back to the United States at the invitation of Union Theological Seminary in New York. But amid much inner turmoil, he soon regretted his decision despite strong pressures from his friends to stay in the United States. Bethge shares a letter Bonhoeffer wrote to Reinhold Niebuhr (a professor at Union Theological Seminary):

> I have come to the conclusion that I made a mistake in coming to America. I must live through this difficult period in our national history with the people of Germany. I will have no right to participate in the reconstruction of Christian life in Germany after the war if I do not share the trials of this time with my people . . . Christians in Germany will have to face the terrible alternative of either willing the defeat of their nation in order that Christian civilization may survive or willing the victory of their nation and thereby destroying civilization. I know which of these alternatives I must choose, but I cannot make that choice from security.[3]

Leading from your soul means living your life with the convictions of your faith as guiding principles for the decisions you make and the actions you take. Additionally, it's a sensitivity to engaging the conversations that help lead people closer to God. It's modeling a life that is marked by recognition that whatever our level of leadership, we still submit to God's guidance in our lives. And soul (or spiritual) leadership nods to the prevailing theme that leadership is servanthood first. We cannot lead others where we are unwilling to go ourselves.

Just as we learned in our exploration of self-leadership, spiritual leadership starts with leading ourselves in this area and then learning to lead others in this way. In the midst of leading from our heart, mind, and strength, we also have to be intentional about finding ways to lead others spiritually. It is the distinctive that sets you apart as a faith-based leader.

Soul (or spiritual) leadership nods to the prevailing theme that leadership is servanthood first.

Henry and Richard Blackaby wrote an entire book dedicated to the subject of spiritual leadership beginning with this premise: "When God finds people willing to serve as he leads them, the possibilities are limitless. People everywhere are looking for someone to lead them into God's purposes, God's way. People will follow spiritual leaders who know how to lead them according to God's agenda."[4]

It's easy to compartmentalize our lives. Work gets our daytime hours. Family receives our evenings and weekends. God gets Sunday. But as much as we like to subdivide our lives, our faith should not be segregated from our work. Yes, we need to be mindful of respecting the cultures of the organizations we work for, and we should not attempt to convert everyone to our faith or condemn others who don't share our beliefs. However, if our faith is real, it cannot be separated from how we carry out our daily lives. Whether you lead in the marketplace, in ministry, in school, or in your home, as a person of faith you have a responsibility to integrate your faith with your work. You can't separate the two. James challenged us with the question, "What good is it, my brothers and sisters, if someone claims to have faith but has no deeds?" (James 2:14).

Our soul is our moral compass. It's the part of us that longs to know God (Psalm 42:1). From the decisions we make, to the actions we take, to the conversations we engage in, all of these will be infused by the living, breathing presence of God. To try to compartmentalize our faith will only serve to stunt our leadership. Following Christ is who we are, and it should overflow to our leadership.

Soul-full Decisions

"We believe people are more important than the bottom line and that honoring God is more important than turning a profit."[5] That's a big statement from a man who in 2014 was number 96 on the Forbes 400: The Richest People in America list.[6] David Green is the founder and CEO of Hobby Lobby, which he described in a 2012 op-ed piece in *USA Today* as "one of the nation's largest arts and crafts retailers, with more than 500 locations in 41 states."[7] For Green, his faith has informed his decisions as a business leader since the days of his simple start-up in a garage some forty years ago.

From keeping stores closed on Sundays allowing employees a day of rest to paying full-time employees 80 percent above minimum wage, Green and his family have led the daily decisions of their organization with the intention of, in his words, "running their business in harmony with God's laws."[8] In 2012, Hobby Lobby made the difficult and controversial decision to file a lawsuit against the government because the new health care laws required employers to cover the cost of emergency contraceptives, which Green said was "contrary to our most important beliefs."[9] Green's faith has informed his decisions as a leader, and he believes that God has honored that commitment.

For many of us the decisions and consequential actions we face may not be as extreme as Bonhoeffer's or as controversial as Green's, yet we make decisions daily for the organizations and teams we lead that require faithfulness to the principles that guide us. Whether it's a seemingly small and insignificant issue like whether to be honest about being late for work, or a more demanding problem like whether to cover up a poor investment, every day we are met with decisions that challenge our integrity. As people of faith, we must filter every decision we make through the lens of what is God-honoring.

Most important, decision making needs to be processed this way not only because how you handle even the simplest of decisions nourishes your own spiritual health and growth, but also because how you handle them speaks volumes about your character and integrity to those you lead. Your actions are being observed and monitored every day by the people around you. Collectively the good and bad decisions you make are adding up and affecting your influence with them. It's a bank account that neither you nor they are intentionally monitoring daily, but it is compounding and creating either a positive or negative balance.

Soul-full Actions

A leader's life is not his or her own. Every move you make is watched, studied, mimicked, followed, or criticized. How do your actions support your belief system? How do you conduct your business? How do you treat others? How do you value your time as well as others' time? As a spiritual leader, you must define the God-honoring attributes of a follower of Christ and then consider whether your daily actions display these qualities well.

Todd was a professing Christ-follower. In fact, he had devoted the majority of his life to vocational ministry. When I met him, he had spent over thirty years working on staff at various churches in a variety of different positions. But Todd's actions and his words were grossly inconsistent. He prayed lofty prayers in King James language but then barked at his wife for not having dinner ready on time. He would serve all morning at church on Sunday and then berate the waitstaff at lunch after the service. It was embarrassing to be with Todd. You were always uncertain of what would agitate him, and episodes at a restaurant made me want to crawl under the table and hide.

Sometimes I fear that we as believers think that God is only with us when we summon him in prayer, a pseudo-genie in a bottle who appears on demand. But what if we operated with the understanding that God is always with us? And he's with us not to be watching but to be with us, to unite with us, to partner with us. Brother Lawrence, a lay brother in the Carmelite monastery in Paris, was said in letters compiled by Father Joseph de Beaufort to believe that "our actions should unite us with God when we are involved in our daily activities, just as our prayer unites us with Him in our quiet time."[10]

Brother Lawrence never aspired to lofty positions, and in fact he spent the majority of his life serving in the kitchen of the monastery. He is remembered, however, for the way in which he lived out those simple actions. Brother Lawrence's legacy intrigues me because while he lived a very ordinary life as a kitchen helper, he was sought out by many for spiritual guidance and wisdom. Years after Brother Lawrence's death, Father Joseph de Beaufort, later vicar general to the archbishop of Paris, compiled the letters and conversations of Brother Lawrence into the book *The Practice of the Presence of God*, which is widely read by Christ-followers today, some three hundred plus years after his death.

Brother Lawrence understood that his faith spoke loudly through his actions. His life exemplified this passage from 1 Peter, chapter 3: "But in your hearts revere Christ as Lord. Always be prepared to give an answer to everyone who asks you to give the reason for the hope that you have. But do this with gentleness and respect, keeping a clear conscience, so that those who speak maliciously against your good behavior in Christ may be ashamed of their slander. For it is better, if it is God's will, to suffer for doing good than for doing evil" (vv. 15–17).

As leaders, we have a tremendous opportunity to influence others through our actions. And it's the seemingly simple things that can have the most profound effect. How do your actions unite you with God and in turn communicate to others that your faith influences your whole life?

Soul-full Conversations

What does your language convey? I was once a part of a team that could be a little careless with our language. They were great people who I genuinely loved working with, but in the safety of a select group we would engage in inappropriate conversation. It wasn't uncommon for the group to chase a trail of gossip or digress into juvenile humor. Repeatedly, I was convicted by scriptures such as this: "Do not let any unwholesome talk come out of your mouths, but only what is helpful for building others up according to their needs, that it may benefit those who listen" (Ephesians 4:29).

I was certainly guilty of participating from time to time, but more often than not I remained quiet in those conversations rather than speaking up to address my concerns. As leaders, we have the responsibility to speak up and guide the direction of conversations in a God-honoring way. James 3 gives some strong cautions about the danger of our words and suggests that if we can control our words, we can also control our behavior.

Our language matters. In fact, our language is a good indicator of our spiritual health, as the Bible explains: "A good man brings good things out of the good stored up in his heart, and an evil man brings evil things out of the evil stored up in his heart. For the mouth speaks what the heart is full of" (Luke 6:45).

Our words and conversations tell others what we value. If gossip, coarse language, complaining, or criticism is quick to your lips, it will affect your spiritual influence with your team.

Submission and Humility

One of my guilty pleasures is the popular TV show *Revenge*. The main character, Emily Thorne, seeks revenge for those who framed her father for a terrorist attack, resulting in his imprisonment and death. Emily devotes her life to ruining the lives of those responsible. However, in her attempt to play God and seek justice, Emily continues to experience loss and heartache. The more she attempts to control the situation, the more miserable she becomes. While *Revenge* is a fictional drama, it reminds me that too often I attempt to play God with my circumstances. In my need to control and manipulate outcomes, I forget to submit to God's authority.

When we lead from our soul, we recognize that ultimate authority doesn't reside with us. We are a part of God's plan, but we are not God's complete plan. We were not designed to handle deity or celebrity. Our egos can't handle it. When we grasp the importance of our submission to God, humility is a likely by-product. As leaders, we wrestle the difficult tension of having some authority but not all authority. Pastor Obed Martinez, lead pastor of Destiny Church in Indio, California, says, "Authority comes with submission. We must lead with the authority of a shepherd and also with the humility of a sheep."[11] Pastor Martinez reminds us that while we as leaders have been given authority to be shepherds, we must also remember that we are still sheep under the authority of the Great Shepherd. When we forget that we are sheep, we become arrogant, unbalanced, and unhealthy as leaders.

Submission and humility must be anchors to our leadership, yet they are countercultural to popular leadership philosophy. The common perception of leadership, especially in the marketplace, is that leadership is power and rank. As spiritual leaders, we know that Jesus taught that the last will be first and the first will be last. Wise souls recognize that we are always under the authority of someone and that we must operate in mutual submission to those we lead and those who lead us. Leading under the authority of someone else provides a covering of protection both spiritually and practically that every leader needs.

Hebrews 13:17 emphasizes the responsibility for both shepherd and sheep: "Obey your leaders and submit to them, for they are keeping watch over your souls, as those who will have to give an account. Let them do this with joy and not with groaning, for that would be of no advantage to you" (ESV). As followers, we're instructed to obey and submit, which enables our leaders to lead with joy. And at the same time, leaders are reminded that they will have "to give an account" for how they lead. The weight of that responsibility should humble us. Leadership carries a spiritual responsibility to "watch over . . . souls" and "give an account." For leaders, submission and humility go hand in hand. We submit to the authority we're under, and we humbly lead those we're responsible for.

Service with Courage

Great leaders serve. They recognize everything they do isn't for them. Bonhoeffer displayed this best when he chose to return to Germany to endure the Nazi terror with his people rather than stay out of the fray in America. He knew he would have little influence if he didn't go through the horror with them. He literally served to his death.

Leadership is a life of service. It's a recognition that your primary responsibility as a leader is to pour into the lives of those you lead more than you expect them to serve you. This is the opposite of our instincts. Our human nature and our cultural habits have programmed us to expect that the further up we go in the organization, the more others below us are designed to serve us. In most workplaces this is a common expectation, and it is even considered appropriate. It's interns who make the coffee and associates who are assigned the unseemly tasks.

For clarity, if you are the intern or the young associate, you should expect to do the grunt work. You should be

Leadership is a life of service.

willing to serve by doing the menial tasks. It's in those things that you'll learn the ropes and earn the influence for greater opportunities. You, too, need to be willing to serve in whatever way you're asked.

It's a familiar image: that of Jesus washing the feet of his disciples. We've seen pictures portraying this significant moment, and we've read the gospel accounts of it numerous times. As Jesus did in many other ways throughout his life on earth, he chose to perform the unseemly task of washing the disciples' feet in order to serve others. He didn't have to do it. No one expected him to pick up the basin. I suspect he didn't even think twice about it. He saw a need and an opportunity to serve, and it was as natural as breathing to assume that responsibility.

Serving should be natural for us as well. When we feel resistance to taking on seemingly ordinary or insignificant tasks, we have all the more reason to push ourselves to do them. Although it may not be necessary for you to make the coffee, or it may not be the wisest use of time for you to organize the files, always be willing to do it if necessary. The attitude or intention of the heart is the mark of a spiritual leader who understands that the soul of a leader is first and foremost always to serve.

Get Wisdom

I live in a culture where the life of the mind is highly valued. The intellectual horsepower of the corporate executives, attorneys, venture capitalists, and educators that I find myself working with on a daily basis is staggering. The thirst for knowledge is insatiable. Surrounded by some of the most brilliant minds of our generation, I am challenged to continue to grow. And while knowledge is important, wisdom is *essential* for spiritual leaders. Knowledge is information that we get from experience or education. Wisdom is the ability to apply that knowledge in order to make sound choices and navigate life's circumstances.

King Solomon, said to be the wisest man who ever lived, exhibited "a consuming passion for knowledge and wisdom." If King Solomon were alive today, he would fit right into our Silicon Valley culture. *Halley's Bible Handbook* also notes, "He lectured on botany and zoology. He was a scientist, a political ruler, a businessman with vast enterprises, a poet, moralist, and preacher."[12] Solomon's résumé is extensive, yet the greatest legacy he left for us was his writing on the importance of wisdom in our lives.

Wisdom may very well be the most important trait we should seek to develop as leaders. We can't possibly account for every leadership situation we'll face; therefore, wisdom and prayer are the best resources at our disposal. In his book *Give and Take*, business professor and organizational psychologist Adam Grant writes, "Wisdom is the ability to make sound judgments and choices based on experience."[13] But where does that leave us when we have limited experience? Is wisdom reserved only for our twilight years?

While there is no doubt that wisdom grows with age and experience, wisdom is available to us now. Proverbs 4:7 says, "The beginning of wisdom is this: Get wisdom. / Though it cost all you have, get understanding." Get wisdom. A simple and direct statement that seems more easily said than done. Grant provides more context to the idea of wisdom gleaned from experience: "It turns out that the number of life experiences has little to do with the quality of those experiences. According to the data, between ages 25 to 75, the correlation between age and wisdom is zero. Wisdom emerges not from experience itself, but rather from reflecting thoughtfully on the lessons gained from experience."[14] Wisdom is gained by learning from our experiences. We must study, learn, and grow from the experiences that have shaped our lives thus far. It's self-leadership in action.

But there is another element to growing in wisdom that often escapes us. The pursuit of wisdom can easily become a driving achievement. With evidence of wise decisions we can begin to take pride in wisdom. This is where spiritual leadership makes a marked difference for the extraordinary leader. Proverbs 11:2 warns, "When pride comes, then comes disgrace, / but with humility comes wisdom."

On the heels of a successful season of multisite leadership at Cross Point Church, I took a job helping with multisite leadership at Menlo Church. I had extensive knowledge from my experiences at Cross Point and therefore dove into my responsibilities at Menlo with great confidence and, it would also be safe to say, great pride. While I certainly had knowledge that was applicable to my new environment, it was presumptuous to think that I had the wisdom for this new responsibility. Wisdom is never haughty. Wisdom applies past knowledge and experience while remaining humble in new circumstances.

James 3 gives us further clarification on the importance of wisdom: "Who is wise and understanding among you? Let them show it by their good life, by deeds done in the humility that comes from wisdom. . . . But the wisdom that comes from heaven is first of all pure; then peace-loving, considerate, submissive, full of mercy and good fruit, impartial and sincere" (vv. 13, 17). Wisdom is marked by humility, and it's evidenced by the fruit of the spirit actively portrayed in our lives. Spiritual wisdom is countercultural. This wisdom isn't an attempt to prove what we know; it's an attempt to portray what we love.

James 1 tells us that if we lack wisdom, we need to ask God for it and he will give it to us. That's a tremendous promise and incredibly good news for those who want to lead well. Get wisdom.

I've prayed for wisdom for as long as I can remember because I know that I desperately need it and also because it seems like the responsible thing to do as a leader. But what if praying for wisdom is not the greatest prayer we can pray? What if we've missed a significant point in our prayers for wisdom?

While praying for wisdom for ourselves is critical as leaders, equally important is that we pray for wisdom for those we lead. Honestly, this important component of leadership wisdom did not occur to me until I was reading through the New Testament journeys of Paul. As a church leader, I find Paul's influence with the early church quite fascinating. His life is a case study in the earliest form of multisite church leadership. Each epistle begins with words of encouragement, instruction, and prayer. And while I'd read these pages numerous times, his words to the church at Ephesus in Ephesians 1 carried a new perspective for me:

> I keep asking that the God of our Lord Jesus Christ, the glorious Father, *may give you the Spirit of wisdom and revelation*, so that you may know him better. I pray that the eyes of your heart may be enlightened in order that you may know the hope to which he has called you, the riches of his glorious inheritance in his holy people. (vv. 17–18, emphasis added)

Paul prayed specifically that God would equip these leaders with wisdom. Paul didn't pray, "God give *me* wisdom so that I can give them good direction." No, he prayed that God would give the Ephesians wisdom and revelation to navigate the challenges they were facing.

In Proverbs 2, Solomon teaches us the value of wisdom: through wisdom we will understand the fear of the Lord, find the knowledge of God, and understand righteousness and justice. "When wisdom enters your heart, / And knowledge is pleasant to your soul, / Discretion will preserve you; / Understanding will keep you, / To deliver you from the way of evil, / From the man who speaks perverse things, / From those who leave the paths of uprightness / To walk in the ways of darkness" (vv. 10–13 NKJV).

As leaders, we naturally feel the responsibility to give direction and provide wisdom for those we lead. I often pray that God will give *me* wisdom so that I can lead others well, but Paul approached this differently. Paul didn't pray that God would give *him* wisdom to lead others better. He prayed that God would give *the Ephesians* the spirit of wisdom and revelation.

I can't help but wonder if the reason that Paul prayed so deliberately for wisdom for the Ephesians was that he had no other choice. Writing while in prison, Paul knew his influence and opportunities for communication and direction were limited. Perhaps those limits forced him to approach his leadership from a completely different perspective. In praying for the spirit of wisdom for the Ephesians, Paul was praying for so much more. He knew that with wisdom would come all the promises from Proverbs 2.

What if rather than attempting to impart wisdom to those we lead, we begin praying for wisdom to enter their hearts? What if we are secure enough in our leadership to know we are not needed for the wisdom we bring, and we pray fervently that God gives wisdom to our teams? In this we begin to demonstrate the focus of leadership that is other-centric rather than me-centric. In praying for wisdom for those we lead, we are ultimately praying for God to equip them to elevate themselves to greater heights of leadership and influence.

Spiritual Leadership for You

I've worked in both the corporate world and in ministry for nearly equal amounts of time. Perhaps I made an assumption, and maybe you have too, that working in ministry would make my spiritual walk easier. I would, after all, be talking about God frequently when I made my office in a church building, right?

While some would assume that maintaining your spiritual health is easier in ministry, others would claim that it's actually more difficult. Their argument is that because you are engaged in faith conversations, Bible study, and frequent prayer as work-related activities, you do not allocate enough time to do these things for your own spiritual growth and development. In full-time ministry it's easy to engage in spiritual practices for job performance rather than for the purpose of growing in Christlikeness.

Because I've had my feet in both the marketplace and the ministry, I tend to believe that both are difficult for different reasons. Spiritual formation is challenging to pursue consistently regardless of our circumstances. So wherever you lead, the important principle is that your spiritual leadership needs purposeful attention. Once again, you can't lead others where you haven't been yourself. Here are some questions to consider.

What does spiritual formation look like for you?

How do you best connect with God?

Do you pray, reflect, study, and revel in God's beauty
regularly?

Do you have opportunities to engage in spiritual
conversations with other believers?

When do you most feel like you're experiencing spiritual
growth?

Being able to answer some of these questions is important in creating a foundation for the spiritual dimension of your leadership. Following Jesus should make us look different. Others should take notice. As spiritual leaders, we should lead in a compelling and different way. Do love, joy, peace, patience, kindness, goodness, faithfulness, gentleness, and self-control (Galatians 5:22–23) mark your life?

Leading from our soul can be subtle but incredibly distinctive to those around us.

Measuring our spiritual growth is complicated. There is not a documented formula. There is not a clean and easy ten-step process. That's not how Christ is formed in us. Spiritual growth is unique and individualized for each one of us. A great online resource called SoulPulse was developed with this very tension in mind. You can take this online spirituality survey, which is part of a research study, by visiting www.soulpulse.org. According to the sociologists and psychologists who administer the study, "It explores the role of spirituality in everyday life and how it relates character, health, well-being, and daily circumstances. It also gives participants a way to grow personally by learning more about their own spirituality."[15] This is where self-leadership collides with spiritual leadership. We must be willing to do a healthy self-evaluation of our spiritual growth. To assume that our spiritual health doesn't affect our leadership is ignorance.

Spiritual Leadership for Those You Lead

Have you ever had people call, text, or e-mail to simply tell you that they're praying for you? For no particular reason? You were just on their mind and they felt prompted to pray. I have a friend who is amazing at this. Although we live thousands of miles apart, she always seems to know when to let me know she's praying for me. Every time she does this she earns influence. Her sincerity in praying simply because she cares gives her spiritual leadership in my life.

Our spiritual influence with others will be as diverse as our own personal spiritual growth, but here are a few ways that you can consider being more deliberate in your spiritual leadership:

Pray for those you lead. Richard J. Foster, in his book *Prayer*, said this: "If we truly love people, we will desire for them far more than it is within our power to give them, and this will lead us to prayer."[16] Additionally, prayer opens our hearts to others. When we pray for someone, we choose to see him or her as human, in need of God's grace.

Praying for your staff members connects your heart to them. When you're intentional about praying for those you lead on a regular basis, you find yourself more sensitive to concerns they raise, family dynamics they mention, and sensitivities they expose. You might ask more questions about how they are doing, what they are stressed about, and what they are excited about. When you're praying for someone, you desire to know more detail to equip you to adequately pray.

Depending on the circumstances, you may or may not let people know that you pray for them. For people who share your faith, you can encourage them by asking what or how you can pray for them. If you ask them such questions with sincerity, offering to pray for them can build trust.

For those who don't share your faith, you may or may not offer to pray for them. You might choose to pray for them without sharing this information, but there might be other occasions where it is appropriate to share. I once heard the story of a salesman who ended every sales call with the question, "How can I pray for you?" It frequently caught his clients off guard, but once they realized he was being sincere, they would open up and share a burden they were carrying or a crisis they were enduring. This simple inquiry about a prayer opened a door for deeper conversation that turned a business task into a moment of vulnerable human interaction.

Serve those you lead. As humans, we naturally serve those we love. My sister is pregnant with her first child, and even while this baby is in the womb she is doing everything she can to serve the baby's best interests. When her little boy arrives, I have no doubt that she will serve him night and day. It's difficult to serve if we don't love. In serving, we see heart and soul leadership collide. Our heart dimension of loving others meets the spiritual dimension of service.

Is serving others the primary motivation of your leadership? Entire books have been written on the importance of leading with the heart of a servant, so we're not going to do the topic justice in this short section. However, knowing and understanding your motives for leading are essential for leading well. As we consider our spiritual responsibility in leadership, we must evaluate our willingness to serve others.

If we, as followers of Jesus, aim to become like him, we must evaluate his life. We must study what he modeled, and in studying him we quickly discover that he served. He washed his followers' feet. He prayed and watched over them while they slept. He healed the sick. He slowed down for the woman who touched his robe. He didn't delegate these tasks. He performed them and served the people.

Servant leaders consider themselves less and consider others more. Author and management expert Ken Blanchard shares this: "Servant leadership is easy for people with high self-esteem. Such people have no problem giving credit to others. They have no problem listening to other people for ideas. They have no problem in building other people up."[17]

Model it for those you lead. We must be what we want others to be. An unknown writer wisely observed, "True leaders are not those who strive to be first but those who are first to strive and who give their all for the success of the team. True leaders are first to see the need, envision the plan, and empower the team for action. By the strength of the leader's commitment, the power of the team is unleashed."

My friend's five-year-old daughter was recently sitting at the kitchen table diligently writing in a notebook. When her mom asked her what she was doing, she proudly proclaimed, "Writing a book like Miss Jenni." I had no idea my five-year-old little buddy was aware that I'd written books, but her little watching eyes had picked up on it. Without even realizing it, I had modeled an activity that she sought to emulate.

"The three most important ways to lead people are: . . . by example . . . by example . . . by example," claimed theologian and philosopher Albert Schweitzer.[18] Our example matters. We see this all the time with children. The people in our lives are always watching and observing. They consciously and subconsciously are picking up on what we value by what we do, how we spend our time, what we talk about, what we praise, and what we criticize. Every action is observed, and it's our responsibility as leaders to understand that.

Knowing that others are watching, we must be conscious of what we're modeling because we're always leading by example. Mahatma Gandhi gave the theory greater vision when he said it this way: "Be the change you want to see in the world." That's the privilege and responsibility of leadership, and if our spiritual life is important, we must ensure that we're modeling it.

Spiritual leadership is most consistently modeled in our character. It's less about what we say and more about how we live. Do you love, serve, and give to others? Are you kind, generous, and intentional about investing in others? Do your family and friends see patterns of faith such as regular church attendance and prayer time? Do the rhythms of your life reflect time spent with God? Although you don't need to be touting to everyone your early-morning devotion time, as people get to know you, they start to realize what you value. Does your staff know that you're not available one day a week because you practice Sabbath? It's amazing how loudly it speaks to others when you don't send e-mail or receive calls one day each week.

Dangers

As a female leader in the marketplace and ministry, I have faced some challenges regarding how to succeed without selling my soul. Because women have encountered obstacles and often still deal with the glass ceiling, I've found myself mulling through titles such as *The Girl's Guide to Being the Boss (Without Being a Bitch)* or *Nice Girls Don't Get the Corner Office*. Rather than feeling the intended "girl power" of these books, I found myself conflicted. This business-savvy, no-nonsense, make-a-way-for-yourself prescription didn't align with my spiritual convictions. What about love, joy, peace, and patience? What about servant leadership?

But these conflicting thoughts aren't relegated just to women. Hundreds of business books prescribe tactics that demoralize others to make a name for yourself. As tempting as it is to adapt to the world's way of getting ahead, remember Jesus' simple teaching, "The last will be first, and the first will be last" (Matthew 20:16). This scripture provides us insight into the way Jesus taught us to live and what he expected us to value.

Jesus' way is countercultural. Choosing to align ourselves with the character of Christ will always win in the long run over the cut-throat tactics of the marketplace. Living a life of love, joy, peace, patience, kindness, goodness, faithfulness, and self-control will get attention. It looks different. People want to be valued and respected, and when that is consistently how you treat them, you are practicing spiritual leadership whether or not you ever quote a scripture or are given the opportunity to share your faith more specifically.

Living It Out

I once interviewed a candidate for a role at one of the churches I worked for, and the candidate was quick to tell me that he was uncomfortable with prayer and spiritual conversations in the workplace. I respected his honesty in sharing this, but I also felt sorry for him. While not every work environment will be conducive to spiritual conversations, one of the great joys and privileges of working for a church is spending your day with others who share your faith values. To not engage your spiritual self, especially in an environment that encourages spirituality, is unfortunate.

Even if you lead in a culture where it is not appropriate to express your faith views in the workplace, don't leave your spiritual self outside the office door. First Thessalonians 5:17 reminds us to "pray continually." As you prepare for a meeting, work on a report, or anticipate a difficult conversation, take a few moments to ask God to help you in these situations. As you face leadership challenges, study God's Word to learn how leaders in Scripture navigated leadership moments. One of my favorite Bibles for general reading and study is John Maxwell's *Leadership Bible*. Notes and stories are placed throughout, giving leadership principles and insight into stories in Scripture.

Developing as a spiritual leader provides a number of benefits for our overall leadership health:

Divine guidance. Our attentiveness to how our spiritual life works itself out in our everyday life reminds us of our humanity. As leaders, we sometimes tend to slip into assumptions of power or false illusions of control. We can begin to take credit for God's work in us and through us and miss the significance of divine guidance. As believers, we must rest in God's sovereignty and trust that he is in control. We are simply stewards. When leading from our soul is working in tandem with all our leadership dimensions, it provides grounding and anchoring for our leadership impact. We are emotionally positioned to rest in God's sovereignty rather than anxiously try to control every outcome.

Confirmation of our calling or purpose. Spiritual leadership keeps us connected to the sense of calling or purpose that first informed our passion to pursue leadership. There are many leadership responsibilities that won't always feel directly aligned to the core of our calling. For example, part of my job is to oversee the IT department. I actually know very little about IT and have to engage additional energy to lead through problems or concerns that arise in this area. If I'm not careful, I can find myself frustrated by the minutiae of the details, and I can lose sight of how this important department connects to the bigger picture of the ministry I work for and ultimately to the calling I believe God has designed me for. In this case, well-functioning IT systems enable staff members to be good stewards of their time, devoting their focus and energy to the ministries in which they work rather than experiencing the frustration of poor technology.

Connection through prayer. Spiritual leadership cannot occur if we as leaders are not connected to God. In his book *Too Busy Not to Pray*, Pastor Bill Hybels challenges the culture of busyness that leaders face. He says, "Most Christians allow busyness to rule the day. Which, if you ask me, is the unrivaled archenemy of spiritual authenticity. Busyness is akin to something the Bible calls *worldliness*—getting caught up with society's agenda, objectives and activities to the neglect of walking with God." Additionally, he notes, "The heart and soul of the Christian life is learning to hear God's voice and then developing the courage to do what he asks us to do."[19]

Our calling and our responsibility as leaders is too great to not take to heart the impact of spiritual leadership in the areas where we lead. Our faith equips us with an extra dimension of leadership that unlocks wisdom and power that would otherwise be unattainable. It would be a shame if we lived our lives as leaders disconnected from this source.

Questions for Reflection

- How much is your faith involved in your work?
- If leadership is a life of service, how could service become a greater part of your work?
- Do you currently pray for wisdom for your staff?

CHAPTER 6

LEAD WITH ALL YOUR MIND

It is not enough to have a good mind; the
main thing is to use it well.

—René Descartes

Leonardo da Vinci is often regarded as one of the most brilliant minds of all time. Famed for being a painter, sculptor, architect, musician, mathematician, engineer, inventor, anatomist, geologist, botanist, and writer, da Vinci demonstrated through his life and work the enormous capacity that our minds have for learning and thinking.

We know our minds are valuable. Dr. Caroline Leaf, a cognitive neuroscientist who has devoted decades of research to "help[ing] people develop and change their thinking and subsequent behavior,"[1] says that our mind is "the most powerful thing in the universe after God, and indeed, fashioned after God."[2]

What does it mean to lead with our minds? Our minds are where we think and reason. They are the processing centers where we take in information and organize it, enabling us to make decisions and choices. Leading with our minds is critical because our decisions and choices affect not only us but those we're responsible for leading.

Our minds influence our leadership because they equip us to strategize and make decisions that will guide our organizations and those we lead. Our minds enable us to learn, and it is the application of that knowledge, combined with the discernment from the spiritual dimension, that produces wisdom.

Another way to discuss leading with our minds involves engaging the managerial dimension of leadership. Management and leadership are not synonymous nor are they completely disparate. Management is a function of leadership that can often be downplayed. In recent years management has taken a backseat in theories of leadership, with many leadership experts suggesting that leadership is better than management.

I understand the sentiment behind the argument: leadership is certainly more inspiring than management. And to only manage, without drawing on the other dimensions of leadership, can leave followers feeling controlled and uninspired. But to abandon management as an element of leadership is a mistake. Management is the method by which great leadership is executed. Management takes a leader's instincts and inspiration and puts them into action. Management is the stewardship engine that drives leadership. Management is the engaging of our minds toward action.

Great managers get stuff done! They move the ball down the field. In his iconic business book *Good to Great*, Jim Collins talks about the "flywheel concept."[3] Great managers are always looking for ways to get the flywheel moving. They understand the power of momentum, and they know it takes hard work, determination, focus, discipline, and accountability to make it happen.

By definition, management can be summarized by three words: discipline, stewardship, and accountability. *Dictionary.com* defines *manage* as

To bring about or succeed in accomplishing,
sometimes despite difficulty or hardship
To take charge or care of
To handle, direct, govern, or control in action or use[4]

In other words, management is

Discipline
Stewardship
Accountability

Management provides the "what" and the "how" for the "why" of your organization. In his book *Start with Why*, Simon Sinek explains this connection: "Everything you say and everything you do has to prove what you believe. A WHY is just a belief. That's all it is. HOWs are the actions you take to realize that belief. And WHATs are the results of those actions—everything you say and do: your products, services, marketing, PR, culture, and whom you hire."[5] When we manage well, we help the entire team put feet to the vision. Management helps us realize our beliefs—the "why" of the organization.

What does management look like when it's demonstrated every day in our organizations and teams? Let's look at each of these three elements of management.

Discipline

Retelling the story of two teams of adventurers in 1911 on a quest to be the first people in modern history to reach the South Pole, Jim Collins and Morten T. Hansen explain in their book, *Great by Choice*, the "20 Mile March" principle that caused one team to succeed and the other team to fail.[6] The successful team lived by one simple principle: to hike twenty miles every day whatever the obstacles. Some days would be easier than others, but the hikers' steady commitment to an achievable goal allowed them to realize success. In much the same way, managers must create the 20 Mile March principles by which their organization will run. These are the systems and strategies that will allow you to carry out the vision.

The management dimension of leadership is the 20 Mile March of leadership influence. Methodical. Steady. When we engage our minds, we create systems that maintain the organization for the long haul. And those systems provide discipline and endurance in tough seasons.

In one of the organizations that I worked for, we had several 20 Mile March principles that we lived by in regard to finances: we saved 10 percent of every dollar we received, we gave 10 percent to charity, and we maintained three to six months' operating expenses in reserves. These simple principles were guidelines that provided stability for the entire team. In good times we barely gave this saving and giving strategy a thought. Our plenty didn't make it painful. But in lean times it took the discipline of management to hold us to this commitment. The faithfulness to our 20 Mile Marches allowed us the financial stability to realize dreams and continue to live out the vision.

Managerial leadership defines the systems and strategies that will help the organization carry out the vision. Extraordinary leaders not only define those systems and strategies but also hold the team accountable to them in good times and bad.

Managerial leaders are also continuously on the lookout for how to maximize the gifts of the team for the future. They want not only to see the organization endure but also to see individual staff succeed and be effective for years to come. Managerial leaders know that the effort it takes to match employees' gifts with the right job responsibilities is critical to the success of the organization.

Extraordinary leaders put intentional time and effort into building review processes and performance management systems that create effective dialogue between employees and their managers. They look for ways to allow staff members to grow in their strengths and areas of interest. They continually evaluate organization charts and team dynamics to find the best combination of talent with task. Extraordinary leaders understand that when the gifts of staff members are aligned with their actions, the organization will achieve maximum effectiveness.

Discipline is what transforms ideas into accomplishments. Managerial leaders understand the importance of discipline, and they are dedicated to keeping themselves and the team committed to the essential elements that lead to long-term success.

Stewardship

Stewards are people who care for someone else's property. They oversee, protect, and care for what is entrusted to them. That's also the management responsibility of a leader. As people of faith, we are accountable as stewards on behalf of two different owners: (1) God, who created it all and entrusted it to us, and (2) the organization for which we work.

A familiar passage in Matthew speaks to the responsibility and the consequences of stewardship. Jesus told the story of a master who entrusted three servants with different amounts of money. One of the servants was given an amount comparable to one hundred years' wages, the second was giving forty years' wages, and the third was given twenty years' wages. This was an outrageous sum of money for three men who had very little resources of their own. What an amazing opportunity to prove themselves! While the master was away, the first two servants went to work and both doubled the amount they were given. But the third did nothing. In fact, he dug a hole in the ground and hid the money. He literally buried his treasure.

I'm quick to criticize the third guy. "Seriously, you just buried it! You were given an amazing opportunity. Don't squander this!" But then I put myself in his shoes. He's a servant. He's at the bottom of the corporate ladder. He's not used to a lot of responsibility, and he's fearful of messing it up. When the master confronted him about why he buried it, he said, "I was afraid" (Matthew 25:25). Paralyzed by fear, he was unable to steward the treasure he was responsible for.

That's the way it is for you and me as well. How many times

does fear paralyze us and prevent us from stewarding what's been entrusted to us? Each of these servants was given a responsibility that was probably much greater than they'd ever experienced before. The first two rose to the challenge, but the third allowed fear to hold him back from experiencing his greatest opportunity for growth and freedom. We do this too.

Maybe it's accepting a new job that requires a leap of faith, a cross-country move, and a new team culture. Maybe it's investing in the launch of a new location or expanding a division of your organization. Maybe it's reorganizing your team and realigning the structure to prepare you for the future. Will you embrace this new challenge and risk the payoff, or will you sit on your hands, fearful of change, and have nothing to show for it?

Maybe doing nothing isn't as big an issue for you. In fact, if you're like most leaders, your drive and determination push you to always be looking for more. The problem is that you're never content with what you have right now. So instead of stewarding well what you have, you're always comparing where you are to where others are. You focus your attention on the opportunities you don't have rather than seeing the potential of the ones you do. In this way, you are burying what exists in hopes of acquiring something better. The important principle about stewardship is that it's not about the amount we've been given; it's about managing well what we have.

When we're intentional about stewardship, we build the guidelines that equip our teams to make good, consistent decisions about how to best manage the resources of the organization. Managing resources goes far beyond money. It means stewarding the people, the time, the tools (facilities, equipment), and the money.

Stewarding People

The stewardship of people is the highest calling of the leader. Our primary responsibility is developing the best in others and calling that out for the good of both them and the organizations they serve. So even when we're operating from the managerial dimension of leadership, the underlying motivation is others. We're building infrastructure that helps provide direction and framework for the people we serve. We're giving them the tools to make good decisions.

> There is something divinely beautiful that happens when we as leaders can pair the gifts of an individual with the needs of the organization.

In addition, we have the unique privilege and responsibility to steward the gifts, talents, and calling of each of the people entrusted to our leadership. There is something divinely beautiful that happens when we as leaders can pair the gifts of an individual with the needs of the organization. This is a managerial practice that has truly spiritual implications. We have the privilege of partnering with God to assign his people the roles and responsibilities that allow them to live out their God-given best.

Stewarding Time

One of my annual New Year's traditions is to review my calendar. I revisit the past year to see what I did. What was continuously out of balance? Did I spend enough consistent, quality time with my spouse and my family? How about my friends? Did I take breaks and vacation well? Did I have consistent time with

God? Did I make time for serving others? What was my routine for working out? Was there enough fun in my schedule?

Stewarding our time gets tricky. Time is a commodity that is difficult to quantify. We live in a culture that values busyness. But being busy doesn't always reflect good stewardship of time. We can be busy doing a lot of things that don't actually help us accomplish the things we're responsible for. David Allen, author of the best-selling book *Getting Things Done*, has this to say: "What you *do* with your time, what you *do* with information, and what you *do* with your body and your focus relative to your priorities—those are the real options to which you must allocate your limited resources. The real issue is how to make appropriate choices about what to *do* at any point in time. The real issue is how we manage *actions*."[7]

As I reflect on my work calendar, I consider the pace of meetings. Was I always in a hurry? Did I give appropriate amounts of time to the right people? Did I say yes too much or no too much? Were my regular meetings the most effective way to accomplish the goal? What was missing that would allow the team and me to operate better?

Taking all these questions into consideration, I review my schedule for the new year. I consider new goals and objectives and build a new calendar that supports them. As leaders, we need to understand that the stewardship of time starts with the habits we create for ourselves and extends to applying the same principles to our organization as well as individual staff members. Rarely will the same meeting schedule, or lack of one, work for your organization forever. Growing organizations require growing structures and systems. Every once in a while you just have to blow it all up to reset what you really need.

In one season of leadership, I felt like our team was bogged down in too many meetings. The intention for each meeting was good, but we had drifted toward not using the time in those meetings as effectively as we once had. We were busy meeting, but we weren't really getting much done. So for a month I canceled all meetings. I wanted to see how team members would get information and get their jobs done without the structure. Certainly, it was chaotic at points, but the real needs surfaced, and we quickly identified which meetings were actually necessary and which ones had become obsolete or ineffective.

How well do you understand what it takes for each of the people you lead to do his or her job? Although it's incredibly unpopular (at least when you first suggest it), I recommend having your entire staff do a time log for a two-week period. Ask all staff members, yourself included, to keep a log in thirty-minute increments of how they spend their time each day. Initially employees will feel like this is a watchdog tactic and be resistant, but push through their frustration and help them see that the goal is to help you better understand what it takes to do their jobs. The benefits go both ways. Employees will probably have some aha moments about time that gets chiseled away by unnecessary interruptions, and you will gain a greater understanding of the numerous details that go on behind the scenes in their everyday work.

While stewarding time reflects the obvious need to make sure our teams are working wisely, it's equally as important to steward time in a way that creates a sustainable rhythm of work for your team. Do you build in time for fun and time for celebration? After intense seasons that require extra focus, energy, and commitment, do you set aside a period for rejuvenation? Do you set aside time for your staff to dream, plan, and anticipate the future?

Stewarding Stuff

The other leaders of our young church plant and I would often dream of the promised land—a building all our own. For years we met in a gritty elementary school cafeteria to hold our Sunday services. Sundays began at 4:30 a.m. and, four services later, concluded at 8:00 p.m. Those were grueling days, but we had hope for our own facility one day. The glory of an idea has a tendency to shine brighter than reality.

Eventually we did get our own building, in fact, a couple of them. And with that great privilege of ownership came even greater responsibility. Leaky roofs to repair, toilets to unclog, stained carpet to clean, lawns to mow, lightbulbs to replace, lost keys to duplicate, copiers to repair because they repeatedly jam at the most inopportune moments. We traded some long days in a stinky cafeteria for a list of tasks that seemed completely unrelated to our mission as a church. I found myself living with the growing tension of managing tasks that felt disconnected from our purpose.

Leaders manage a lot of stuff. It might not be buildings, but at a minimum you manage your personal stuff—cars, homes, clothes, computers. Stuff also includes phone systems, database networks, file-sharing tools, project management systems, and more. If you don't build strategies for managing the stuff, it will bog you down. Broken copiers and poor database systems may be time-consuming and expensive to deal with, but the energy that gets wasted in lost time and frustration is even more costly to you and your team. When you find yourself in a role in which it's your responsibility to steward stuff, don't take for granted the long-term impact on the mission that occurs when teams are derailed by the seemingly trivial.

Stewarding Treasure

I'll never forget the day I signed a check for $1 million. We had just purchased a building for our organization and I felt the weight of the new responsibility. My big-girl pants were on, and I was drowning in them. When I first began my career, marketing budgets felt more like monopoly money. As one cog in a three-hundred-person company, I was disconnected from the reality of the ledger line. Budgets were a number on a report, and my effort to stay within my allocated budget was motivated solely by how the balance affected my performance review. But as leaders, we learn that stewarding the resources of the organization means life or death to that organization.

If you remember, 2010 was a tough economic year. The economy still hadn't rebounded from the recession, and to make matters worse, Nashville, where I lived at the time, had been devastated by a historic flood. Resources at the church I worked at were lean, as they were for most nonprofits in town. After a particularly tough board meeting at which our leaders acknowledged the difficulties we were facing, I was tasked with looking for places to cut back and helping us wade through the tough months ahead.

Every penny counted, and I had to motivate our team to keep performing at a high level while at the same time cutting spending. Some of those conversations were grueling. I said no much more than I said yes. I disappointed more people than I pleased, but in the end we made it through the year without having to downsize staff. Notably, one of the most trying seasons of leadership for me was met with very few pats on the back or thank-yous. I had kept the ship afloat, but outside our core leadership very few people had realized the brink we were teetering on.

Stewarding our resources as leaders involves keeping an eye

on how every financial decision affects every part of the organization. And it means stewarding those resources the same way in good seasons and bad. I mentioned earlier some of the 20 Mile March principles that we put in place at that same organization. Having principles for how you manage your money in the good times makes it easier to manage in the bad. If we hadn't been faithful to the principles in times of plenty, we wouldn't have had the financial foundation to hold us steady in a lean season.

Leaders understand this, and they are willing to make consistent and disciplined financial decisions at all times. They keep their eyes on the big picture. They account for the unexpected.

A big part of financial stewardship is creating systems for accountability regarding how spending occurs within your organization. How are reimbursements processed? Who approves what expenses? Do you have parameters for business meal expenses? Do you require several quotes before you purchase items?

Money is a tool that helps the organization accomplish its vision. It's not a necessary evil. It's essential, and you as the leader are responsible. Admittedly, many of us find ourselves in positions of leadership with responsibility for budgets and financials, but with little experience and training in these areas. Those of us who are born with the desire to influence people often lack the passion for manipulating Excel spreadsheets and analyzing financial reports. That's okay. A rare few will excel at both, but the rest of us have to figure out how to embrace the responsibility without drowning in a sea of digits.

Not being good with numbers is not a reasonable excuse to dismiss your responsibility. Study. Learn. Seek mentors. You don't have to understand how to run the accounting software to understand what the data means. Hire great people. If you lead a small organization and you're not in the position to hire a full-time accountant to manage your finances, there are organizations that provide accounting services with well-qualified individuals. There are resources available. Don't allow fear of the unknown to keep you from tapping into resources that will help you succeed in this area. Ignorance is no excuse for leaders.

Stewardship Instills Confidence

Kurt was eager to assume his new responsibility as executive director of a well-known, long-standing nonprofit. The organization had a reputation for being well funded, and he was excited to lead a team that appeared to be unbound by financial limitations. Little did he know what he was walking into. Years of unstable financial stewardship had created a culture of fear and scarcity. Staff members were known to hoard and protect budgets. Teams inflated budget needs for fear of not getting the resources they really needed. While the organization had better reserves than other companies Kurt had worked for, the culture exhibited an unhealthy view of resources because of the lack of stewardship throughout the years.

While the responsibility of stewardship is weighty, good stewardship inspires hope and freedom. Good stewards inspire trust in those they lead. The steadiness of great discipline frees teams to deliver their best, confident that leadership has a good handle on the foundational issues.

Stewardship Inspires Action

Great managers inspire actions in others. Action breeds action. Momentum, by definition, is movement. When you initiate activity that is worthwhile and accomplishes the vision, it motivates others. (And if it doesn't, you need to take a long, hard look at whether you've got the right people on your team.)

In his TED Talk, leadership expert Simon Sinek explains, "All the great and inspiring leaders and organizations in the world . . . they all think, act, and communicate the exact same way. And it's the complete opposite to everyone else." Sinek continues, "There are leaders and there are those who lead. Leaders hold a position of power or authority, but those who lead inspire us. Whether they are individuals or organizations, we follow those who lead not because we have to but because we want to. We follow those who lead not for them but for ourselves."[8]

What Sinek is expressing is that great leaders inspire people with "why." They don't just tell you "what" or "how"; they give you a reason to believe, a reason to buy in that is more substantial than the practical one. They appeal to your heart and your desire for purpose.

When great managers embrace the responsibility of stewardship, they are transforming management principles from the "what" and "how" of business to the "why." Stewardship provides a more substantial reason to attend to details that may seem monotonous or cumbersome. Stewardship gives purpose to our managerial tasks. It causes us to perceive spreadsheets and systems not as unnecessary bureaucracy but as support networks for accomplishing our goals. Stewardship is where the visionary (strength) dimension of extraordinary leaders collides with the managerial (mind) dimension.

Stewardship Accepts Responsibility

In Luke 12, Jesus shared a parable about preparedness. The servant who was put in charge of the owner's estate began to question when or if the owner would be coming back. As a result, he began to take his responsibility for granted. He threw parties, got drunk, and abused everything for which he was responsible. He lost sight of what he was taking care of and for whom, and he abused the privilege of leadership. The parable concludes with this statement: "From everyone who has been given much, much will be demanded; and from the one who has been entrusted with much, much more will be asked" (v. 48).

Stewardship is a significant responsibility. As leaders, we are entrusted with people, time, tools, and treasure. The more of these things we're given, the greater the responsibility becomes. We can't deny it. We can't escape it. We can't ignore it. We can't abuse it. We must remember who has entrusted us with this steward-ship, and we must be faithful. We can't escape our responsibility by indulging in moments of immaturity. When we understand our responsibility to be good stewards, we feel the weight of it. It compels us to give our best to what we've been given.

Stewardship Maintains Alignment with Vision

Every few months when I pull into the car dealership for my regular oil change, the mechanic offers a complimentary align-ment check for my car. Of course, I say yes. It's free, right? And inevitably every two or three visits, the mechanic explains that my car is just a fraction out of alignment and then proceeds to provide a laundry list of reasons why if I don't do an alignment today all these other things on my car will be out of whack. It's just a matter of time.

I'm always confounded by how easily the car goes out of alignment. It could have been a pothole in the road or a curb that got a little closer than I thought. A slight bump that lasted an instant and that I can barely recollect has the potential to cause significant damage later on down the road if I don't give it attention.

Alignment is critical. It's our job to do regular alignment checks for the organizations we lead. Misalignment happens with the simple things—a slight alteration to a procedure; an overlooked step in a process; an employee who didn't complete the entire onboarding process or, worse, was not put through an onboarding process; a customer complaint that was dismissed rather than addressed; or a coaching moment that was passed over because you didn't have the energy to engage in a difficult conversation.

In a *Forbes* article, Joseph George writes, "As organizations grow, one of the greatest impediments to continued success is lack of alignment. . . . *Alignment* is the key ingredient to success, because without it, the most perfect strategy in the world will never come to fruition."[9] Everything we do in our organization is either keeping

> **Everything we do in our organization is either keeping alignment with the vision or it's derailing the vision.**

alignment with the vision or it's derailing the vision. There is no neutral. And you as the leader must do the work to maintain alignment. You must be relentless about coaching your staff to adjust the fractional discrepancies.

Accountability

During his two terms as mayor of New York City, Rudy Giuliani led with the philosophy "I'm Responsible." In an effort to make himself and his team accessible and accountable, he held monthly town hall meetings where citizens were given the opportunity to ask questions and raise concerns. Giuliani and his staff's goal was to either respond immediately to the issue or develop a plan to do so.

Management is the accountability quotient of leadership. Dreams are just dreams, without action. First, we must learn the discipline to hold ourselves accountable, as we discussed in chapter 3. But then, and perhaps even more challenging, we must learn to hold others accountable. In his book, *Leadership*, Rudy Giuliani expresses his thoughts about leaders and their responsibility to be accountable: "More than anyone, leaders should welcome being held accountable. Nothing builds confidence in a leader more than a willingness to take responsibility for what happens during his watch. One might add that nothing builds a stronger case for holding employees to a high standard than a boss who holds himself to even higher ones."[10] By creating a monthly forum for direct feedback, Giuliani kept himself and his team accountable to the people they served.

The management dimension of leadership involves leaning into others to get their best work. Respect and kindness shouldn't be absent, but management should be practiced with authority and reasonable expectations. One of the great privileges of leadership is that we are able to help others accomplish feats that they didn't think they had in them. By holding people responsible for predetermined and agreed-upon outcomes, we help them achieve greater things than they might have accomplished on their own.

Let's look at some principles for creating a culture of accountability:

Clarify expectations. Accountability begins with clarity. You can't hold yourself or others accountable to expectations that haven't been clearly defined. John Maxwell believes, "Everyone likes clarity. Even people who are not bottom-line thinkers want to know the bottom line."[11]

Begin by considering yourself. What are your goals? What are your dreams? The more clearly you define the path for your life, the more likely you'll be able to realize those goals and dreams. As a leader, you bear the responsibility of leading others to set goals that will help them fulfill their responsibilities. Every day you are clarifying the needs that will help you, the organization, and each individual team member further the vision of the organization.

Remember, you are the chief vision caster, and the clarity you provide for the activities that support the vision is the engine that's driving the vision car. The vision looks fancy, but it's useless without the engine that drives it.

Follow up. Once you've defined the expectations, you must also create pathways for follow-up. Repetition is essential. The old adage "The squeaky wheel gets the oil" has survived for a century or so because there's truth to it. Managers must at times be the squeaky wheels. We must be the loudest and most consistent voice when it comes to the organization's priorities.

You must determine both when and how to follow up. Once your priorities are established, you need to determine the best environments for follow-ups as well as their frequency. To help yourself be consistent, create a system to keep the priorities front and center. Whether you use a digital system like Evernote or old-fashioned paper and pen, creating a process for follow-up is essential.

It's also important to understand that our personalities will dictate different styles in our management. Relational types may be more inclined to have an organic, conversational style of follow-up. Systematic types will have routines and structures that support their follow-up process. Whatever your style, you must have a method that enables you to be consistent with follow-up. For example, both relational and systematic types can keep a list of priorities that each staff member is focused on. With a system that keeps the right priorities on your radar, you can then facilitate follow-up based upon what works best with your personality.

Measure results. Focus on results more than process. If you've clarified your expectations, you can leave room for how an employee accomplishes a goal. Brian Dishon, the multisite director for Cross Point Church, leads his team with what he refers to as the "Equals 4 Theory" of management. When assigning a project to a staff person, he makes sure that he and the employee have agreed that their goal is to arrive at 4. And they take time on the front end to define what 4 is: 4 is not 3, it's not 2, and it's not 10. It's 4. Then he allows the employee liberty as to how he or she arrives at the goal of 4. The employee might get there by 3 + 1, 10 − 6, or 2 × 2. As long as the employee arrives at 4, the agreed-upon expectation, they both win.

Often we as managers tend to manage employees by pushing them to reach their goals or accomplish their tasks by the same methods we would employ. While there are occasions when this may be necessary, often we lead this way simply because a certain method worked for us. When we set clear goals and have a consistent follow-up plan, we can focus on measuring results rather than on mandating a particular process.

Evaluate ROI. I've learned valuable principles from my

time in corporate leadership and ministry leadership, especially in regard to stewardship. The greatest difference, however, has been in how we evaluate the stewardship of people, time, money, and stuff. There was a term that I first became familiar with in the corporate world: ROI, or return on investment. Every decision we made was evaluated against what the return would be on our investment. Because we were selling a product, we could quantify nearly every decision by how many units would be sold. I assumed, however, that when I transitioned to ministry, it would be impossible to evaluate ROI. How do you assign a profit to life change?

Imagine my surprise when I was networking with some peers from another church, and they explained how they measure ROI on every decision. I was intrigued. ROI in ministry might not translate to dollars and cents, but whatever product you "sell," you must define what the return on investment is for everything you steward. When you invest in training a staff member, what return do you expect from that investment? When you purchase new gear for the production team, how is that going to support the goals and mission of the organization? When you don't hold your staff accountable to office hours, do you know how much money you've paid out in salary for squandered time?

A Dangerous Mind

Arrogant. Pompous. Know-it-all. These are some of the descriptors that we assign to people who lead with their minds but little else. When we lead with our minds but with the absence of heart, soul, and strength, others perceive us as someone who just has something to prove. We can be condescending and brash.

Sometimes insecurity is at the core of this attitude; we need to prove that we have the knowledge to succeed. Other times the cause can be a lack of self-awareness and emotional intelligence. Sometimes truly brilliant people are trying to help share what they know, but without a balance in the heart, soul, and strength equation, their mind-fullness comes across as just pure arrogance.

Perhaps the reason we shy away from management discussions in modern leadership is that we've felt the pain of being dehumanized by our managers. Tasked with goals and responsibilities that overwhelm and frighten them, great leaders can become anxious taskmasters. As leaders, we must remember what Sir Ken Robinson shares in his book *Out of Our Minds: Learning to Be Creative*: "Human organizations are not actually mechanisms and people are not components in them. People have values and feelings, perceptions, opinions, motivations, and biographies, whereas cogs and sprockets do not. An organization is not the physical facilities within which it operates; it is the networks of people in it."[12]

We must keep in mind that while our minds are critical to leadership, we can't lead without the other dimensions of heart, soul, and strength. When we are imbalanced in our managerial leadership, we can become impersonal. This is an area in my leadership that I have to watch very closely. I have a strong bias toward action, and I can lean into the managerial components of discipline, stewardship, and accountability to an unhealthy degree. It's not uncommon for people to comment that I'm "all business all the time."

Another caution to be aware of in our managerial leadership is that when our minds are engaged in problem solving and planning, we can become a predictor of doom, spinning off every worst-case scenario. We must learn to plan for and be mindful of potential consequences without being the wet blanket smothering ideas and vision. There is a balance between being wise and being paranoid. Once again, this is where our leadership functions best with heart, soul, mind, and strength equally active.

Mindless Leadership

And then there are those who fear that strategy, planning, process, and systems are too "corporate" for their leadership situation. For fear of being too bureaucratic, they avoid strategic thinking and instead feel their way through decisions. This mindlessness leads to confusion and complacency.

For those of us who are leaders in ministry, mindless leadership can happen when we place well-intentioned but disproportionate attention on spiritual leadership. Prayer and Scripture should certainly be key to our leadership, especially when we lead in a church or a faith-based nonprofit; however, often we can be inclined to throw out strategic thinking, believing that God will provide divine inspiration in the absence of intentional thought on our part. Second Timothy 1:7 (NKJV) tells us that God gives us a sound mind, a mind capable of discerning decision making.

A Healthy Mind

When our mind and managerial leadership are balanced well with the other dimensions of leadership, we inspire disciplined cultures where processes are well-defined, systems and structures are clear, and boundaries are understood. Stewardship is an important value, and it means that our staffs are trained and developed, we manage our resources effectively, and we instill confidence and inspire action. Accountability is valued rather than avoided, expectations are clear and respected, and results are aligned with the vision and direction. Leading well from our mind provides the structure for our heart, soul, and strength to flourish.

Questions for Reflection

- Which element of managerial leadership are you strongest in: discipline, stewardship, or accountability?
- What steps could you take to be a better steward of the people you lead?
- What systems or processes could you create to provide better accountability?

CHAPTER 7

LEAD WITH ALL YOUR STRENGTH

The visionary starts with a clean sheet of
paper, and re-imagines the world.[1]

—Malcolm Gladwell

Ryan couldn't quite pinpoint why he was so discontent. He loved his job. He loved his team. He had joined the company nearly a decade earlier, compelled by the vision that the founder and CEO had for developing his fledgling company. While it was a lateral move from his seat at the executive table of a prominent corporation to his position at this unknown start-up, Ryan had been convinced that something special was about to happen, and he had happily accepted the new chair. The first five years had been a whirlwind. Rapid growth, constant hiring, and all the demands that come with both had kept Ryan motivated and on his toes. There was never a dull moment, and the wins the company was experiencing added fuel to the already-accelerated pace they were running.

But in the last few months, Ryan had been keenly aware that something was missing. The company was still growing and expanding, but the gains didn't come with as much joy as they had in the past. It felt as if the machine was running the staff rather than the staff driving the machine. If he was honest, Ryan wasn't even sure everything management was doing was really what it had hoped to achieve. It was all good, but it felt void.

For a while Ryan kept thinking it was him. Maybe he needed a good, long vacation and a fresh perspective. It wouldn't hurt to take a break. Although there was never a good time, he would just need to make it a priority. But even after a much-needed vacation and a few fresh ideas, Ryan quickly realized something was still off.

Eventually he reached out to Paul, the CEO. Paul understood Ryan's concern and admitted that he even wrestled with it himself. Encouraged that it wasn't just him, Ryan pressed further: "Paul, where do you see us going? What's next in your mind? What are you dreaming about these days?" Paul paused for quite some time and, with an emptiness in his eyes, responded, "Ryan, I don't know."

Ryan left the office that day with a heaviness he hadn't experienced in the last ten years. It made sense that he was wrestling with such unsettledness. Paul had lost a vision for the organization, and that loss of vision was affecting everyone and everything around him. The strength of a vision will either carry your team or break your team. In this case, the lack of strength was eroding things very quickly.

"If people can't see what God is doing, / they stumble all over themselves; / But when they attend to what he reveals, / they are most blessed." This is *The Message* paraphrase of the familiar

King James Version of Proverbs 29:18, which says, "Where there is no vision, the people perish" (KJV). When we lose God's way, we stumble. Our job as leaders is to help point the way. Vision is the foundation for our strength as leaders. In our heart, soul, mind, and strength framework, strength is anchored by visionary leadership. Great visionary leaders inspire strength by keeping hope and possibility in front of themselves and those they lead.

It's been said that the first task of the leader is to define reality. The second is to map out where you're going. The strength comes from an assurance of the future. When Paul could no longer define where they were going as an organization, Ryan lost confidence. There was no longer a strong vision for him to follow. When a leader isn't confident of where he or she is leading, those following feel the weakness.

As a little girl, I loved helping my dad with projects. My dad's hobbies typically involve a significant level of home repair. As a kid, I thought that nothing seemed beyond his scope of capability. Knock a wall down and build an extra room? No problem. Rewire the electrical or reroute the plumbing? Piece of cake.

As his diligent follower, I was at the ready to hand him a tool, much like an assistant to a surgeon. I never doubted Dad's ability to pull off the task at hand. In looking back, I think it had a lot to do with the strength of the vision that Dad communicated. He always had a plan and he confidently conveyed it.

Holy Commodities

At the Global Leadership Summit in August 2013, Bill Hybels challenged the one hundred thousand leaders who were watching to understand the importance of vision. "Visions are holy commodities. Treat them with the utmost respect," he pleaded.[2] As the leader of one of the largest churches in the nation and the founder of the Global Leadership Summit, which trains and equips millions of leaders, Hybels understands the significance of vision. He has led through lean seasons and seasons of plenty. He has cast vision well, and he has cast vision poorly. He knows that the strength of leadership rests upon the shoulders of a great vision.

What Makes a Vision Strong?

Hope

When we as leaders are following a vision directed by God, Hebrews 6:19 reminds us that we can be secure in God's promise and that our hope in God's fulfillment of that promise is "an anchor for the soul, firm and secure." Conversely, Proverbs 13:12 says, "Hope deferred makes the heart sick." When vision is lacking and hope is lost, we lose heart. We often talk about the importance of vision casting for leaders, but perhaps we need to reframe it as "hope casting." Casting a hope-filled vision provides strength for ourselves and those we lead.

Possibility and Potential

Strong visions help us see possibility and potential. Great leaders use their influence and power to help calm nerves and change people's perceptions by alleviating fears and providing hope. They reframe reality in a way that makes it palatable.

Visionary leaders understand how to be a bridge from reality to possibility. We're all inclined to naturally be either dreamers or doers. Dreamers live in ideas whereas doers live in reality.

The strength dimension of an extraordinary leader is achieved when you've learned to be the bridge between both. Followers can't follow a dream that seems disconnected from reality, but they also will not be motivated to follow a leader without a plan. Strength of leadership is found in the ability to make connections to possibility.

What Does a Strong Vision Look Like When It Is Lived Out?

Bring Out the Best in the Team

Strength of vision helps others believe not only in the possibility of the goal ahead of them but also in their ability to be a part of it.

Author, speaker, and human rights activist Christine Caine shares her thoughts about how she casts a vision to her team at A21, an organization whose goal is to end human trafficking:

> You can't separate your passion and your heart from what you do. It's easy to keep vision alive when people are passionate. If I can create a compelling picture of the future and create fantastic pathways to seeing that realized, then I think that everyone stays forward looking and we can overcome the obstacles, the hurdles, and the challenges and the circumstances that we're confronting. I think everyone wants to know that there are wins along the way, that my life counts for something, that I'm an important part of it. I make sure that I'm just not imparting a vision but that I'm ensuring that people know they are a part of that vision. I want a vision

Visionary leaders understand how to be a bridge from reality to possibility.

so compelling and so huge that everyone can find themselves in that future, and I think once someone can locate themselves in the future, I don't have to fight to keep them there because the vision itself does the job.[3]

People are inspired to bring their best when they know where you're going and they know how they fit in. As the leader, you must constantly be on the lookout for moments when you can connect the dots from people's gifts and contributions to the vision. When employees help the team excel, point it out and remind them of how it matters for the future. Always look for ways to affirm that you see them with you for the long haul. This both encourages and inspires your team to stick with it.

One employee at a thriving nonprofit was often assured by his leader that he "would always have a job with the organization"; however, his leader couldn't define how his strengths could serve the organization in the future. It's no wonder that the individual moved on. His leader was unable to provide a vision for how his gifts strengthened the team.

See the Big Picture

Leaders with strength of vision always have their eyes on the big picture. Their job is to see further than others see. Most team members are in the trenches, focused on their area of responsibility. They are not always aware of or privy to how their piece fits into the whole. Therefore, leaders provide much-needed strength to team members by helping them see how each individual role plays a part in the big picture.

When the accounting staff is frustrated with other employees who are not following procedures, take the opportunity to remind the entire staff why faithfulness to the accounting process maintains financial integrity and helps manage resources wisely. Additionally, when the entire staff follows the process, the accounting department can remain focused on its regular responsibilities rather than tracking down missing information. When administrative staff members are feeling overwhelmed by managing schedules and booking travel, remind them of how their accuracy in those details enables the leaders they serve to focus on their own responsibilities. Every time you are able to tie everyday tasks to vision outcomes, you provide immeasurable motivation to teams.

Inspire Confidence

A strong vision that is lived out inspires confidence. When you're leading others to a vision, they must know you believe it can be achieved. If they sense doubt from you, why would they risk themselves to achieve something you the leader aren't even confident of?

An organization that struggled with this dilemma hired me as a consultant. Occasionally I will work with churches or organizations to help their teams develop strategy to accomplish their vision. Nothing is more satisfying to me than to work with an organization to align their team for success. In this particular case, the leaders had a great vision, and everyone on the team agreed that they wanted to work toward that goal; however, they could never get traction toward realizing the vision.

When I initially talked with the CEO about working with this organization, I was puzzled about why it was having so much difficulty—it had a great staff, it had the resources it needed, and it had a leader with a vision. I didn't see any roadblocks until I began spending time with the people and unearthed the lack of confidence that permeated the culture. The leadership doubted some of the staff members, and the staff members doubted themselves and the leadership. No one had confidence in anyone. Until people developed confidence in one another, they weren't going to get any traction toward fulfilling the vision.

This need for confidence is twofold. First, you must be confident in the vision and in your belief that it is what God is calling your team to accomplish at this time. Second, you must be confident that the team and each individual can contribute to accomplishing this goal. If your staff members are uncertain about your belief in them, they will rarely have confidence in themselves. You must believe in your team. If you don't, you need to determine why you don't believe in it and then make a decision about what needs to change. Visions are carried out by teams that believe they can achieve them.

What Do Leaders of Strong Vision Need?

Courage

It takes courage to lead toward a vision. Marketing professionals and entrepreneurs are familiar with something called the law of diffusion of innovation. The crux of the law is that people accept new ideas and concepts at different paces. The innovators (2.5 percent of the population) are the dreamers and the visionaries who define new ideas and are the first to believe they are possible. The early adopters (13.5 percent of the population) are the first group to embrace the ideas of the

Visions are carried out by teams that believe they can achieve them.

innovators. They are followed by the early majority (34 percent), the late majority (34 percent), and finally the laggards (16 percent).

Visionaries are on the front end of the law of the diffusion of innovation. They are the innovators. But if you consider the bell curve of how people adopt new ideas, you can see that it takes work to get everyone engaged. It takes courage to stick your neck out for a new idea and keep championing it until every group engages with it.

Patience and Endurance

If courage gets you started, it's patience and endurance that see you through to a realized vision. Hebrews 10:36 instructs, "You need to persevere so that when you have done the will of God, you will receive what he has promised." When we as leaders are leading others toward a vision that is inspired by God, he will bring that vision to fruition, but the realization of that vision may come at a different pace than what we hope for.

I think of Noah, who spent a hundred years preaching to his generation while building the ark in obedience to God's command. Abraham and Sarah were one hundred and ninety years old respectively when they finally received the promise of a son. Jacob worked seven years and then an additional seven to marry the woman of his dreams. God's timing and God's methods are rarely like ours, but when we stay faithful and patient, he fulfills his promises.

Hebrews 6:10–12 says, "God is not unjust; he will not forget your work and the love you have shown him as you have helped his people and continue to help them. We want each of you to show this same diligence to the very end, so that what you hope for may be fully realized. We do not want you to become lazy, but to imitate those who through faith and patience inherit what has been promised." Living in a culture that is impatient with process, we need to remind ourselves and those we lead that when we follow a God-directed vision, we must also trust his timing. As this verse says, we must not become lazy, but instead stay faithful to the work he has called us to while patiently awaiting the outcome.

Conviction

I went on my first foreign missions trip to San Pedro Sula, Honduras, when I was sixteen years old. I had never been out of the country. I had never been on a plane. I had never been away from home for an entire month. But I felt God calling me to this, and the experience changed my life forever. I've gone on a missions trip nearly every year of my life since then.

Even though traveling to developing areas of the world has become a regular part of my life, the injustices that I've experienced never become common to me. In fact, the most common emotion I feel on nearly every trip is anger. It's difficult to see extreme poverty and not get angry about the injustice.

I get angry at the lack of leadership. When did leaders fail? When did people quit dreaming for a better future? When did they stop envisioning a better existence? Somewhere along the way leaders failed to provide hope, possibility, and opportunity. It's the only thing that explains why the majority of our world lives in poverty. Somewhere a leader failed to take responsibility and lead people to a better future. Somewhere a leader turned a blind eye. Somewhere a leader gave in to corruption. Somewhere a leader became obsessed with power and prestige rather than truly being a servant.

And I'm not just talking about political leaders. Government doesn't fix everything. Great leaders who led movements that changed the face of history emerged without political position. Consider Martin Luther King Jr. or Mother Teresa.

Not every one of us is called to directly support the developing world, but every leader is called to lead a God-given vision. What vision has God given you? What is that thing that keeps you up at night and keeps the wheels of your mind turning? What is that thing you can't stop talking about? As a leader, you must know what your conviction is. Your conviction ultimately defines your vision. If you don't know what keeps you up at night, you will drift from one great idea to the next and never have the perseverance to see a vision to completion. My fear for us as leaders is that we give up too easily if we don't see immediate results. Our need for immediate gratification distracts us from following through on a vision for the long haul.

Patience and endurance are fueled by conviction. Conviction is the mark of a true vision. Conviction puts teeth on a passion.

Focus

Visionary leaders need focus to stay committed to living out the vision. That's why conviction is so important. Conviction provides focus.

Culture is not on our side with this one. If we don't immediately experience results, we're quick to move on to something new. This is a serious challenge for leaders.

Katie Davis has become somewhat of a legend in her hometown of Brentwood, Tennessee. At the age of eighteen Davis traveled to Uganda for the first time. Little did she know the burden God would lay on her heart to help the people she met and the vision he would call her to fulfill. Two years later Davis was living in Uganda. She had personally adopted thirteen children and had started a nonprofit ministry that describes its goal as "to meet the physical, emotional, and spiritual needs of the people of Uganda who need it most."[4]

Davis's story is fascinating and inspiring, but what's even more moving is her focus. Showered with opportunities to write, speak, and share her story with others, Davis is very focused on staying present for and available to the people she feels called to serve. She has given up the comforts of home and sacrificed some relationships and personal joys to stay committed to the vision God has laid on her heart.

When leaders are driven by conviction and focused in their efforts, they will help keep the entire team going in the same direction. Clarity of vision provides the strength the team needs to maintain the alignment we talked about in chapter 6.

What Does a Strong Vision Do?

When Scott Harrison tells you the story behind the organization Charity: Water, you can't help but be compelled.[5] There are hundreds of great organizations focused on providing clean water to the developing world, but when Scott shares his story and his vision, his passion moves you in a different way. While Harrison's personal passion is contagious, he has the stats to back it up. In just seven years the organization Charity: Water raised over $100 million and funded over eight thousand water projects.[6]

Harrison's vision is an example of what great visions do: they propel momentum, and they inspire others.

Protects and Propels Momentum

Focus and alignment protect and propel momentum. A strong vision removes friction and enables momentum. When a vision is reinforced with action, momentum builds. Once the flywheel is moving, vision becomes the energy that continues to propel it.

Conversely, a splintered vision slows the team down. In a planning meeting for the coming year, my team was discussing multiple options for our strategic goals as an organization. The more we talked, the more options emerged. Each department argued the case for why its goal was the most important. After much debate and conversation I realized we had strayed significantly from our overarching vision. We were chasing a number of rabbit trails and losing sight of our key goal or vision. As the leader, I had the responsibility to bring the conversation back to focusing on our primary vision as an organization. We were getting bogged down because we were wasting valuable time and energy with disparate ideas.

Scenarios like this are not uncommon for any team; therefore, the leader's task must be to keep the focus on the driving purpose of the organization in order to protect and propel momentum toward accomplishing that vision.

Inspires the Team

A leader who is passionate about the vision provides inspiration for the team. In an interview with ABC News following Steve Jobs's death, communications expert Carmine Gallo shared this about the role vision played in the success of Apple's cofounder: "Vision is everything. . . . A bold dream attracts evangelists, and no lasting brand can be built without a team of dedicated people who share the vision. Passion fuels the rocket; vision directs the rocket to its ultimate destination."[7] Gallo elaborates on these thoughts in his book *The Apple Experience*: "You simply cannot build an organization that delivers an extraordinary customer experience unless you have a clear vision of the type of experience you plan to offer."[8]

Gallo captured what Jobs embodied: great vision inspires others. It compels people to be a part of it. It's why new product launches motivate lines of people to wait overnight outside Apple storefronts. When you as a leader wholeheartedly believe in the vision of the organization you're leading and/or the product you're selling, it inspires others to believe too. And when people believe, whether they are employees, customers, or congregants, they will pour their hearts into making that vision a reality.

The Danger of Strength

While visionary leadership is seemingly the inspiring dimension of leadership, it doesn't come without its own pitfalls and dangers. Visionary leaders are susceptible to several dangers or barriers that can inhibit them from casting a strong vision.

Not Addressing the Questions

Ask any parent what questions they most dread hearing from their children and you'll probably hear one of these:

"But why?"
"Are we there yet?"

Curious kids ask "why" about everything. They want to understand the significance. They are making sense of their world.

They are beginning to understand how things connect to one another.

And of course any good family road trip is rife with the question, "Are we there yet?" Even the little people want to know where you're going and when you're going to get there. It doesn't matter how many times you've answered it; when they are getting impatient or bored, you can hear it whelming up from the backseat before it even comes out of their mouths.

As adults, we do this too. If we don't understand a decision by our leaders, we often question, complain, or criticize it. If we can't see how the decision connects to what we're doing, we get especially anxious and frustrated.

Few people blindly follow. The stronger your team, the more opinionated its members will be and the more questions they'll want answered. Despite our best intentions to articulate the vision clearly, our teams get distracted by the immediate tasks before them and can forget the "why" behind what we're doing. When it feels like a vision is slow to come to fruition, they're asking when we're going to get there because they've forgotten how traveling this road will lead to our destination.

Strong visionary leaders must remember that vision leaks. We need to anticipate the questions that those we lead will be asking. We must look for opportunities to answer questions before they become frustrations. Visionary leaders look for every opportunity to connect the team's everyday work to the big picture of the vision ahead.

Charisma Rather Than Vision

Another pitfall we can be susceptible to is believing that being a visionary leader means being charismatic. Visionary leaders can be charismatic and gregarious, but charisma is more about style and less about substance. Loud, gregarious leaders with bold ideas and big dreams are energizing for a time. But when these leaders continue to power through, convinced more energy and new ideas will mobilize people, they rarely generate more action; instead they incite greater frustration. Strong visionaries who have no heart for those affected by the vision, or who lack strategic skills or spiritual discernment, exhaust those they're leading.

Often leaders with strong visionary instincts will find themselves frustrated and demotivated because they have difficulty seeing their visions come to fruition. They will often choose to work independently because others "just don't get it." They don't realize that their visionary strength has actually become a weakness because they lack the focus the other dimensions provide.

A *Boston Globe* article titled "The Myth of the Visionary Leader" cites examples of when charisma alone doesn't cut it:

> Take John F. Kennedy, who emerged as immensely charismatic in his campaign and is remembered as an exemplar of transformational leadership. In his book, "The Strategic President: Persuasion and Opportunity in Presidential Leadership," [George C.] Edwards [III] points out that JFK's personal magnetism was not particularly useful when it came to passing legislation. While trying to get Medicare passed, he delivered a televised address to a massive crowd of cheering supporters at New York's Madison Square Garden. But public opinion didn't seem to shift, and the bill proceeded to die in Congress. Later, as Richard Reeves describes in his book on the Kennedy administration, the president was forced to confront the limits

of his rhetorical gifts when, in the aftermath of his 1963 speech in support of civil rights, he saw that racial tension around the country had only escalated.[9]

Casting vision is not about simply being a cheerleader. While there are occasions when that is appropriate or even required, true visionary leadership occurs when a leader inspires others with a plan and also has the track record to follow it through to reality. Vision without action creates pipe dreams. Visionary leaders are not only dreamers; they are doers too. Visionary leaders repeatedly remind those they lead of where they are going and why and develop the plans for follow-through.

Succumbing to Fear, Doubt, and Worry

The team I was working with needed to launch a new initiative. I had led a similar project with another client, so I took the job with great confidence that I could help this team achieve its goal. But it was only a matter of weeks before I started to doubt whether we could really do it. I feared that I had underestimated the challenges, and I worried about whether I could really lead the team to success.

I've yet to meet a strong visionary leader who didn't wrestle with fear, doubt, or worry. It's part of being human. It's part of putting ourselves out there as the leader; we're willing to be the one to go first and lead the way. But if we're leading the way, we're going to run into the obstacles first. And fear, doubt, and worry can become roadblocks if we're not prepared for them. In his book *The Heart of Leadership*, Mark Miller says, "Fear has stolen the future of countless leaders. . . . A fear of failure, fear of the unknown, and even a fear of the responsibility that comes with leadership."[10] If we're not on the lookout for the pitfall of fear, it can become a major roadblock to leading well. If we're wrought with fear, we can't summon the confidence to cast a compelling vision and inspire others to join us.

In my situation, I had to quickly acknowledge the fear I was facing. In order to lead the team confidently, I had to draw on the strength of the vision ahead of us and look for ways to keep moving forward in spite of my fear, doubt, and worry.

Casting Your Vision Instead of God's Vision

Perhaps the most dangerous pitfall we face as visionary leaders is casting our own vision instead of God's vision. We don't plan for this. It's not our intention, but when we grow too confident in our own strength rather than relying on God's power, we can begin to lead from our own vision.

A great example of how casting our own vision can be dangerous shows up in the relationship between King David and the prophet Nathan. David had recently become king. He had conquered Jerusalem and defeated the Philistines. Once he was comfortably settled into the palace, he expressed to Nathan his frustration that he was living in a palace "while the ark of God remain[ed] in a tent" (2 Samuel 7:2). Nathan quickly replied, "Go ahead and do it [build the temple], for the LORD is with you" (2 Samuel 7:3).

This seems like reasonable counsel, right? It appears to be God-honoring. Of course, building the temple for God would be a good priority. But that night God spoke to Nathan and shared with him that his counsel to the king was wrong and that it was not time for David to build the temple. God's plan was for David's offspring to build the temple. Building the temple was not God's plan or vision for him.

Nathan learned an important lesson in this story. He was too quick to speak up and affirm something that seemed like a good plan before he sought God.

Many of us do this in our leadership, especially those of us in ministry leadership. We assume our ministry initiatives are God's plan and direction because they are good and honorable things, when in fact we have not sought God's direction and may actually be leading people toward our vision rather than a God-directed one.

Strength Lived Out

Without vision we flounder. You can have great heart, employ great strategies, and pray with and for your teams faithfully, but if you don't have a strong sense of where God has called you to go, you will flounder as a leader. Followers need someone and something to follow.

In today's culture people long for their work to have meaning. More and more people are pursuing meaningful work. They want to be a part of a mission with purpose. In a *Harvard Business Review* article, Nathaniel Koloc, cofounder and CEO of ReWork, a mission-driven recruiting company, writes, "What talented people want has changed. They used to want high salaries to verify their value and stable career paths to allow them to sleep well at night. Now they want *purposeful* work and jobs that fit clearly into the larger context of their career."[11]

This makes the need for clear and compelling vision even greater. If you want to build and retain a great staff, you have to give people a reason to commit. Young leaders today don't feel like they have time to waste on routine work. They will find someone else with a greater vision if you can't provide them with one. How do we develop strong visionary leadership? What does it look like when it's developed in our lives?

Seek God for the Vision

Ultimately we as leaders have a responsibility to lead others to God's great vision. To do so, we must position ourselves to hear from God.

The Old Testament prophet Habakkuk was desperate to hear from God. The people of Judea were being punished by the wicked Babylonians, and Habakkuk didn't understand why God was allowing it. Eager for vision, direction, and hope, Habakkuk pleaded with God for answers, and he positioned himself in the watchtower as an act of readiness to hear from God (Habakkuk 2:1).

When God responded to Habakkuk, he instructed him to "write down the revelation and make it plain on tablets" (Habakkuk 2:2). Habakkuk knew the vision had to come from God. He knew that as a leader he was powerless to give a vision of hope to the people of Judea on his own. The strength of the vision came from the creator of the vision. Habakkuk knew his role was to be the conveyor of the vision, not the creator. As leaders, we too must remember that our primary purpose is to carry out the piece of God's great vision that we've been entrusted with.

Think Strategically

With a mission "to bring clean and safe drinking water to every person in the world," Scott Harrison began Charity: Water.[12] But Scott knew his vision wouldn't become a reality on its own. With a desire to see more young people engage with charitable causes, Harrison built his business plan differently than most nonprofits do. Employing the strategies of a start-up business and focusing on the power of social media and online technology, Harrison built a business model that enabled the majority of his fund-raising to come through online means.[13]

Visionary leaders engage their minds and think strategically about the plans and purposes they feel God is calling them to. They take seriously their responsibility to steward the vision that God has entrusted to them, and they develop ways to bring that vision to reality.

Be the Chief Reminding Officer

Visionary leaders know that one of their greatest titles is chief reminding officer. We must remind our teams every day of how what they do ties to the vision. Visionary leaders are always looking for ways to connect the dots. While you can formalize parts of your vision casting through mottos that hang on the walls of your office or through other structural organizational systems, you must also personalize every interaction.

When employees do a great job on a project, don't just tell them they did great. Take it a step further and remind them of why their success matters to the vision of the organization. In staff meetings make a point to celebrate accomplishments that support the organizational vision.

Repeat the words of your vision until your team repeats you. The best evidence that your vision casting is working is that your team begins to finish your sentences or mimic your key vision statements.

Avoid the Whirlwind

Every leader feels the tension of dealing with the urgent daily tasks while maintaining focus on the big picture. Being busy is not hard. Being focused is the challenge. In their book, *The 4 Disciplines of Execution*, Chris McChesney, Sean Covey, and Jim Huling call this dynamic the whirlwind versus the WIG (wildly important goals). They explain, "The whirlwind is urgent and it acts on you and everyone working for you every minute of every day. The goals you've set for moving forward are important, but when urgency and importance clash, urgency will win every time." They continue, "Executing in spite of the whirlwind means overcoming not only its powerful distraction, but also the inertia of 'the way it's always been done.'"[14]

Do you know what your wildly important goal is? Do you know what the most important thing you need to do every day is? The more clearly you identify the priorities that will lead to your desired outcomes, the more clearly you'll lead your team. Part of casting vision to your teams is defining the wildly important goal and then providing pathways to see that goal accomplished. You must fight the inertia of the whirlwind and help your teams stay focused on the goal at hand.

Elements of a Strong Vision

The vision will often come easily to you as a leader. Where you want to go will be clear even if how you'll get there may be fuzzy. But it's important to remember that everyone who needs to go there with you may not see the vision as clearly. Remember that leaders see things others don't see yet, and they see further than others see. So in order to cast a vision in a way that helps others see what you see, you need to craft your vision carefully. Here are some elements to consider in casting your vision.

Tell a Story

For a number of years I have sponsored a child through the organization Compassion International. When I signed up to begin sponsoring my child, I received this wonderful booklet of pictures and information about the five-year-old girl who would grow to become an extended part of our family. Without ever meeting her in person, I was drawn into her life because of Compassion's commitment to sharing her story.

Stories make the vision relatable and personal. They create heart connections. They resonate with our human need for connection and community. If you're casting vision for why your product can help others, tell the story of a customer who was affected by it. If you're asking people to contribute to your nonprofit organization, share a story of someone's life that was changed by the work you do.

Be Descriptive

One of the reasons I so quickly connected with our Compassion child was that I received details about her family, her hobbies, and her interests. The organization even described the type of house she lives in and the work her father does. Through its deliberate attention to detail, I was able to envision her life and understand more of her story.

Details matter. When you're casting vision, use vivid imagery. Paint a picture with your words. Match the language to the spirit of the vision. Consider the audience you need to inspire with this vision, and use words that will connect with them. Adventurers want to be challenged. Dreamers want to be inspired. Identify the emotion you want the vision to evoke, and match your language to that emotion.

Be Concrete

Beyond helping me connect to my child, Compassion also helps me understand the impact of my sponsorship. The organization outlines what my donation is helping to fund each month. It provides updates on my child's progress in the Compassion program and at her school. I can be confident that the vision I'm supporting is strong.

In addition to inspiring with story and descriptive language, also remember to provide concrete details. Define tangible results. Give specific details on what the vision will look like when it comes to fruition. Concrete details will be the anchor that connects the vision to reality. You don't want the vision to feel like a pipe dream with no real possibility.

Owning Someone Else's Vision

All of us will find ourselves in situations where we need to embrace the vision of an organization or leader and deliver it as our own. Most of us are not the first-chair leaders responsible for creating the primary vision for the organization of which we're a part. In this case, owning someone else's vision becomes incredibly critical. To own someone else's vision, you must trust, support, and believe in the leader whose vision you need to champion.

Matt worked for a successful ministry organization. By outward appearances the organization was doing great, but Matt wasn't comfortable with some of the new initiatives the CEO was suggesting. After asking some additional questions and clarifying the vision, Matt decided it was time for him to move on. He wasn't personally comfortable with the new direction the ministry was taking.

If you don't trust and respect your leader, you will never be able to convey his or her vision with integrity. You must either work to build trust or choose to move on. It's unfair to you, your leader, the organization, and the other staff members to champion a vision you don't believe in.

If you have questions about your leader's vision, spend time with your leader to clarify it. Again, you can't relay it and help support it if you don't understand it. Be respectful and patient, but make sure you understand it. Odds are that if you don't fully understand it, others won't either.

Vision Casting to Yourself

You understand the importance of vision casting. You know that as a leader you need to cast vision to others. But what about casting vision to yourself?

I've been through numerous seasons in my time in ministry when I have forgotten the importance of remembering the vision myself. I have taken for granted that I need to be reminded of the "why" behind the "whats" just as much as those I lead.

I haven't exactly forgotten the vision. If you asked me, I would rattle it off by rote. But while my head remembers, sometimes my heart forgets. I can get busy doing the "what" of ministry and slowly find my heart disconnecting.

Have you ever been there? As the leader, you are less likely to have others who will consistently remind you of the "why." In fact, you'll more commonly get pestered with questions rather than encouragement, unless you know where to look.

To keep your head and your heart connected to the vision,

you have to create ways to cast vision to yourself repeatedly. Here are three ways that I have learned to do this:

1. **Prayer**. The demands on your leadership often make extended prayer time feel like a luxury you can't afford. This is the easiest way for our hearts to disconnect from the vision and purpose God has called us to. Don't neglect the amazing gift of spending time with God and hearing from him.

2. **Stories**. Whether it's a quick testimony someone shared on a Sunday morning or an e-mail someone penned about a transformative experience, let each story be a reminder of the power of God's vision in action. I keep a file on my computer for e-mails and stories that I've received. On the days when I'm struggling to find significance in my work, a quick read through a few of these stories reconnects me with the heart and the impact of the work we do.

3. **Mentors**. You need people you can go to on the dark days. These might be other ministry leaders, coworkers, or friends, but they need to be people who know how to reinspire you with truth. Beware: they're likely to regurgitate your own words back to you, but that's okay. It's probably exactly what you need to hear.

Author and entrepreneur Seth Godin writes, "The secret of leadership is simple. Do what you believe in. Paint a picture of the future. Go there. People will follow."[15] The vision isn't going to burn brightly every day. Some days it will feel like a flicker, but acknowledge that and create ways to help you reignite it. That's what will set you apart as a leader.

Questions for Reflection

- How strong do you feel about the vision you're working toward? Is there anything you need to do to help you own it more?
- What could you do to more confidently convey this vision to your team?
- What fear, doubt, or worry gets in the way of your vision?

PART 3

THE PRACTICE OF EXTRAORDINARY LEADERSHIP

Leadership is not the private reserve of a few charismatic men and women. It is a process ordinary people use when they are bringing forth the best from themselves and others. When the leader in everyone is liberated extraordinary things happen.[1]

—James M. Kouzes and Barry Z. Posner

CHAPTER 8

PUTTING EXTRAORDINARY INTO PRACTICE

That's what leadership is all about, identifying quality people,
giving them the opportunity and experience to create and
develop to continue to make the company successful. The
best leaders identify and mentor potential leaders. A leader's
most important legacy is the leaders he or she develops.[1]

—**Kenneth E. Strong and John A. DiCicco**

The moment I met Jeff Henderson, I knew he was an extraordinary leader. His reputation preceded him. Numerous other young leaders had raved about Jeff's influence in their life. When I attended a conference session that Jeff was teaching, it affirmed all that I had heard. Jeff was humble and kind in demeanor yet strong and assertive in knowledge. My pen couldn't keep up with the ministry wisdom flowing from his forty-five-minute lecture.

Shortly thereafter, Jeff invited Pete Wilson (the pastor I was serving with at the time) and me to meet with his staff at Buckhead Church. Jeff was eager to learn from us about what we were doing to reach twenty-somethings. Pete and I were both a little taken aback that Jeff wanted to learn from *us*. We needed to learn from him! But the invitation was another example of Jeff's extraordinary leadership in action. Jeff embraces a spirit of constant learning and growing.

The test of real heart, soul, mind, and strength leadership is longevity. Anyone can behave like an extraordinary leader to make a good first impression, but that wasn't the case with Jeff. Over the seven plus years since I first met him, I have talked with several staff members who have worked for him, and they all resoundingly affirm his extraordinary leadership. I've watched his influence increase as he has embarked on more training and equipping for ministry leaders through Preaching Rocket, an organization focused on helping pastors preach better sermons. I've observed him transitioning out of his leadership as campus pastor at Buckhead Church to lead the start-up of North Point Ministries' newest campus, Gwinnett Church. Jeff's life as a leader has demonstrated consistent growth and intentionality to develop as an extraordinary leader.

Heart, soul, mind, and strength are the completeness of our leadership. It's all of who we are working together. When we bring our whole hearts, when we bring our brilliant minds, when we bring our passionate souls, and when we bring our relentless strength to the leadership table, we bring our best selves. One without the other leaves our leadership wanting and incomplete.

Heart, soul, mind, and strength leaders are compelling. They are warm, engaging, confident, and strong. Whenever I encounter one, I become a little agitated because I recognize all the inadequacies in my own leadership. It's not that extraordinary leaders are perfect. Even the greatest leaders among us are still growing and still being formed into all that God desires them to be; however, leaders who lead consistently from heart, soul, mind, and strength are a little further along the leadership development path. They carry themselves with strength and confidence yet without arrogance. They embody what civil rights activist Jesse Jackson described when he said, "Leaders must be tough enough to fight, tender enough to cry, human enough to make mistakes, humble enough to admit them, strong enough to absorb the pain, and resilient enough to bounce back and keep on moving."[2]

Extraordinary leaders aren't leading for themselves. They are leading for others. When we're leading with all of who we are, it becomes less about ourselves and more about those we serve.

How Do We Do It?

So how do we pull it all together? How do we consistently live the life of an extraordinary leader? I look at the life of a leader like Jeff, and I see how far I still have to go. I suspect there is probably a leader in your life whom you aspire to emulate as well. While great role models are helpful and even essential, don't allow yourself to obsess over someone who should serve as an inspiration rather than an idol. Allow this person's strength to serve as something to aspire to rather than a reminder of what seems to be an unattainable goal.

Pulling it all together is a process. And the first step of the process is being aware of your strengths and weaknesses when it comes to leading from your whole self. Are you a stronger heart leader, soul leader, mind leader, or strength leader? Which dimension are you the weakest in?

Here are some steps to take:

- Identify which of the dimensions you are strongest in. Review the assessment you took earlier in the book (see page 11). Ask family, friends, and coworkers which dimensions they see in you.

- Learn more about the other dimensions. Identify people in your life who are stronger in the other dimensions, and begin observing their strengths. In fact, you'll probably discover that the strengths they bring in other dimensions may have been elements that frustrated you in the past. With a fresh understanding of the importance of each dimension, you can begin to learn and appreciate what others bring while you're also discovering ways that you can grow.

- Understand the potential liability of your strength. A gift in disproportion becomes a liability rather than an asset. A *Bloomberg Businessweek* article explains, "We know from more than 30 years of research on high performers in athletics, the military, and business that as stress increases, people tend to overuse their strengths. Under stress the range of people's behavioral responses tend to narrow and they become less flexible and less adaptive to the situation at hand."[3] The overuse of our natural strengths leads to an imbalance that actually hurts our effectiveness.

- Bring people around you who balance your leadership. While you're continuing to grow into all the dimensions of leadership, recognize that your strengths will always lean toward one or two of them. Be purposeful in keeping people around you who balance your leadership strengths. If you're in a leadership seat that involves hiring staff, steward this responsibility carefully. Your staff culture will be critically affected by your intentionality or lack thereof in this area.

Heart, Soul, Mind, and Strength in Balance

We've talked a lot about what it looks like to lead without the balance of heart, soul, mind, and strength. But what does it look like when they're working together? How does our leadership benefit when we've learned to lead from all four dimensions?

As an extraordinary leader, you lead with a grace and confidence that is compelling. People naturally want to follow you because you are easy to respect and hard to ignore. You display genuine, not self-serving, interest in others. You truly love others well. You are smart, strategic, and shrewd. You make wise decisions not so you can be popular but so you can do what's best for everyone involved. You are not afraid of making a decision that might disappoint one person but be better for the whole group. You understand the difference between doing the right thing and doing the popular thing, and you have the courage to do what's right.

As an extraordinary leader, you allow your faith to guide you. Your spiritual life is not separated from your work life. You don't live a compartmentalized life. You commit your work to prayer and feel the weight of the responsibility for leading the people you've been entrusted to lead. You recognize that every ounce of influence is ultimately given by God, and you steward it wisely. You seek God first for direction and guidance. You always have an eye on the big picture. You are committed to charting the course and helping others catch the vision for where you are going. You know the value of leading people step-by-step to seeing this vision come to life. You are patient about reminding and explaining. You are quick to point out milestones along the way. You are a cheerleader and encourager. You lead with all of who you are—heart, soul, mind, and strength.

Passing It On

As we discussed at the beginning of the book, the Great Commandment is "Love the Lord your God with all your heart and with all your soul and with all your mind and with all your strength," and the second-greatest commandment is "Love your neighbor as yourself" (Mark 12:30, 31). Once you've begun to understand what it looks like to lead with your whole self, the next step is to learn how to teach others to lead this way too. Great leaders beget great lead-

Great leaders develop other leaders.

ers. Harvey S. Firestone, founder of Firestone Tire and Rubber Company, believed, "The growth and development of people is the highest calling of leadership."[4] One of the greatest joys and privileges as a leader is to see other leaders grow. We love other leaders well when we are intentional about developing them. This is how we live out the second commandment in our leadership lives.

How do you teach others these skills? How do you replicate your leadership? Great leaders develop other leaders. Once you've defined what heart, soul, mind, and strength look like in your life, you must turn your focus outward and look for ways to develop the leaders around you.

Relentlessly Believe

One of the greatest gifts you can give to the people you lead is belief in them. Too often, we undervalue the people right under our noses. "A prophet is without honor in his own country" is a paraphrase from Scripture that has become an issue that many of us resign ourselves to.

Lynn was a rising star when she was recruited from one company to another. Her new boss saw Lynn's potential and wooed her by affirming Lynn's strengths and potential. Energized by her new boss's level of belief in her, Lynn thrived. She continued to grow, developing her gifts as a leader while also becoming a sought-after expert in her field of work. But after a few years Lynn sensed she had hit the ceiling. She had grown and exceeded the potential her boss had seen in her initially. Lynn had higher aspirations, but in talking with her boss she was discouraged by her boss's inability to see more growth potential for her. Lynn's boss had put the proverbial lid on Lynn's leadership. His inability to see Lynn's further development became the driving reason why Lynn eventually moved on.

When others don't see our potential, it can be incredibly defeating.

You would think Jesus would have been the hometown hero, yet even he was not acknowledged for his gifts by the people closest to him. In Mark 6 we read:

Jesus left there and went to his hometown, accompanied by his disciples. When the Sabbath came, he began to teach in the synagogue, and many who heard him were amazed.

"Where did this man get these things?" they asked. "What's this wisdom that has been given him? What are these remarkable miracles he is performing? Isn't this the carpenter? Isn't this Mary's son and the brother of James, Joseph, Judas and Simon? Aren't his sisters here with us?" And they took offense at him.

Jesus said to them, "A prophet is not without honor except in his own town, among his relatives and in his own home." He could not do any miracles there, except lay his hands on a few sick people and heal them. He was amazed at their lack of faith. (vv. 1–6)

Even Jesus' influence was limited because of the lack of belief others had in him. As a leader, you have the power to make your team members hometown heroes. See the potential they don't yet see in themselves. Be the first to notice them. Create opportunities to stretch them. Identify their gifts and affirm them. See potential before there's proof. Be a part of the unique work that God wants to do in others, and be a catalyst for bringing that to life in them. Sam Walton, the founder of Walmart, once said, "Outstanding leaders go out of their way to boost the self-esteem of their personnel. If people believe in themselves, it's amazing what they can accomplish."[5]

Readily Teach

Great teachers look for every opportunity to make a connection and help their students apply their learning to everyday life. Great leaders do this as well. As you engage with your staff members, look for opportunities to teach them the principles of heart, soul, mind, and strength leadership. Assess your staff members' strengths. Help them understand where they are strong and where they are weak. Teach them the value of heart, soul, mind, and strength working together and in balance. Give them some suggestions for ways they can exercise their weaker dimensions.

And don't forget that one of the best forms of teaching is by example. Share with them your own journey of growth as a leader. Point out times when you've succeeded and also when you've failed to lead from all four dimensions.

Strategically Hire

While balance in heart, soul, mind, and strength are important in individuals, it's also important on teams. In fact, as a team we can achieve balance more quickly than we can as individuals. We are stronger together when we each bring our leadership strengths and value the strengths that others bring.

Each organization I've worked for was clearly stronger in one dimension than in the others. The corporation that I worked for when I was just out of college was very strong in the dimension of mind, one of the ministry organizations I worked for was exceptionally strong in heart, and the other ministry organization was very strong in soul. The reason for being stronger in one dimension than in the others had less to do with vision or purpose and more to do with the personality types of the people the organization hired. Most organizations are likely to reflect the dimension that is most dominant in the senior leader, and that is because the senior leader is going to naturally value that dimension more in hiring and recruiting.

We're inclined to hire others who are like us. This is human nature. We gravitate to people who value what we value. When it comes to leading from our heart, soul, mind, and strength, we're most likely going to be drawn to others who are strong in the same dimensions that we are. If you're a strong heart leader, you're going to connect well with other heart leaders. If you're a strong mind leader, you'll seek out other mind-full leaders. The same is true for soul and strength.

As you recruit and interview, look for team members who will bring strengths in the dimensions that you are weak in as a team.

This tendency isn't inherently bad, but hiring a disproportionate number of people strong in the same dimension will create imbalance in your team. As you recruit and interview, look for team members who will bring strengths in the dimensions that you are weak in as a team.

Purposefully Mentor

Nate's department was growing quickly. Nate and his boss, Chuck, both agreed that it was time to divide up his responsibilities so that he wasn't continually stretched beyond his capacity. Together they mapped out which responsibilities would make the most sense for Nate to keep, and then Chuck began recruiting a leader to head up the new division that was created from the responsibilities Nate would be giving away.

Chuck was excited to tell Nate about the young leader that he intended to promote to the new role, but instead of sharing Chuck's enthusiasm, Nate was skeptical. Chuck paused to reconsider his decision, but he was confident that the new young leader had the instincts and potential for the job, so he proceeded, hopeful that Nate would come around. Unfortunately, Nate never did. Instead of becoming a mentor and support to the new leader, Nate remained distant, critical, and unhelpful. Nate's unwillingness to see the new leader's potential and act as a mentor became a glaring roadblock in his own leadership development.

Mentoring can be a vague concept, so I use it here reluctantly. As I've stated a number of times, development of others is your responsibility as a leader. You must own this. You must constantly be on the lookout for less experienced leaders who you can support and encourage. Nate missed a significant opportunity to help train and develop a younger leader. While Nate was not responsible for personally managing this individual, he had done the job previously, so his experience equipped him to be a great resource. He could have reduced the new leader's learning curve, but he chose not to.

Purposefully mentoring others means keeping your eyes open for leaders a step or two behind you who would benefit from your influence. Look for ways to help developing leaders win. Pave the way for them by giving them helpful advice or insight into situations you've faced before.

Mentoring is less about creating a formalized ongoing relationship and more about making your knowledge available to those who show genuine interest in learning from your leadership journey.

Consistently Coach

Allan was tasked with helping a tired company revitalize its programs. It had failed to keep pace with new technologies, and as a result its customer base was shrinking. Introducing new ideas was essential to turn things around and keep the company in business. Allan had come from another company that had faced similar challenges. He knew what it would take to get this team where it needed and wanted to go. Although the employees agreed with his plan, they were uncomfortable with the process. The new initiatives felt foreign and uncomfortable. Without Allan's continual coaching they were tempted to drift back to their old methods of operation. Although the change didn't happen overnight, Allan and the team eventually succeeded in their efforts due largely to Allan's consistent coaching.

Every interaction with your team members is an opportunity to coach their leadership skills. When you see good, call it out. When you see growth needs, pull people aside and give kind yet specific feedback. Every day is game day. Every meeting is a play in the game.

Great coaches have the perspective of the whole game, the entire field, and all the players. They have a vantage point that the players in the game do not have. Likewise, as a leader, you have a perspective that your staff won't have. Those we lead need real-time feedback that enables them to adjust, improve, and keep playing with all their gifts and strengths maximized and best directed.

Relentlessly Realign

Developing great leaders means constantly positioning them for their best effort. Always be evaluating your staff members to look for better alignment of their gifts and strengths with the needs of the organization. Especially in a growing organization, it is not uncommon to reorganize the staff every twelve to eighteen months. That can feel unsettling at first, but when you've created a culture where your employees trust that your realignment efforts are genuinely for their good, they become much less scared or skeptical of organizational change.

Misalignment will discourage your best leaders. Young leaders with great potential won't stay on teams where their gifts are not effectively utilized. This doesn't mean appeasing every desire and whim of a young leader. Young leaders often don't know what is best for their growth in the long run. But when they know you are for them and working to position them within the organization in areas that will utilize their strengths while at the same time stretching their development, they will engage the process and commit to your development plan for them.

Bravely Break Up

It just wasn't working. I really wanted it to, but I was slowly coming to grips with the fact that Donna wasn't a fit for the job we had hired her to do. She and I were having honest conversations about the challenges. She was really trying. She wanted to make it work, but I knew in my gut we had done all we could. The mismatch of the role and her strengths was starting to put strain on other staff members and creating more confusion. I knew I had to make the difficult decision.

Breakups are inevitable. Despite your best intentions to build a great team, there will be times when you need to part ways with staff members. Sometimes they choose to leave. Sometimes you have to let them go. Letting staff members go has been some of the most difficult work of my leadership life. It is never easy, especially if you're truly leading with all of your heart, soul, mind, and strength. When you're leading with your whole self, you can't help but feel the loss, hurt, anxiety, and fear that accompany transition.

Embrace Seasons

"To every thing there is a season, and a time to every purpose" (Ecclesiastes 3:1 KJV). When I was going through one of my job transitions, it occurred to me that I often treated my employment like I treated my marriage—with the intention of forever. Loyalty is an important thing, but loyalty doesn't always mean forever.

For many things in life there are seasons, and our jobs and careers fall into that category. It's unlikely that we'll have one job for all of our lives. In fact, a number of studies report that Americans will hold at least a dozen jobs in their lifetime.[6] This is why it's important to understand the rhythm of seasons. Some employees will be under your leadership for a short season, and others may actually be with you through several seasons. Recognize that seasons change and that there will be times that employees need to move on whether by your choice or theirs. Additionally, there will be employees who you get to coach, develop, and mentor for a long time, but you may actually be preparing them for a season of growth elsewhere. Likewise, you'll reap the benefit of the time other leaders have invested in the lives of staff members that join your team. Seasons change. Embrace them.

Never Give Up

Not every young leader you invest in will get it. Some won't see the value of your leadership investment, yet others will soak up every word. Some will circle back and thank you later. One of my toughest leadership moments involved transitioning out a staff member that I really enjoyed working with. Although we were known to push each other's buttons, we often did so because we were both passionate about the ideas we held. Unfortunately, this transition was a rocky one. Despite my best intentions to handle it wisely, I made several mistakes. When I should have leaned in to engage, I held back out of insecurity and fear.

When this employee left, I gave her space because I knew the relationship was strained. While I was probably right in that assumption, time allowed the wounds to heal. A few years later I was speaking at an event and connected with some people who currently worked with my former employee. They raved about her leadership and how grateful they were for her influence in their lives. A short while later I received an incredibly kind note from this former employee thanking me for all the things she learned from me under my leadership. She cited the lessons that she learned and explained how she was applying them in her new role. She acknowledged the awkward terms we parted on and owned her part of that dynamic. It was one of the most meaningful letters I've received in my leadership journey thus far. For all that I did wrong, God still redeemed what was good and restored a sour relationship.

That story reminds me that our leadership efforts don't return void. We may not always reap the fruit of them immediately, but God is at work. Some of us plant the seeds, some of us water, some of us cultivate, and some of us harvest. As a leader, you will play different roles for different people. Seize the season you're in. Own the moment you have, but never give up on what God is doing through your life as a leader.

Questions for Reflection

- What next step do you need to take to develop as an extraordinary leader?
- Who is a young leader whom you should purposefully develop?
- What else do you need to consider as you develop yourself and others to be leaders of heart, soul, mind, and strength?

YOU WERE BORN TO BE EXTRAORDINARY

For I am confident of this very thing, that He who began a good work in you will perfect it until the day of Christ Jesus.

—Philippians 1:6 (NASB)

I'm a perfectionist by nature. I'm never satisfied with the status quo. I long for better and best, and I rarely let myself off the hook. I push myself. I beat myself up. I get impatient with my lack of growth. I grieve when I fail as a leader. I feel the weight of leadership every day. It's a burden that I carry. It's weighty. And honestly, sometimes it smothers me. It is difficult for me to find grace for myself. The urgency of the calling bears down on me, and I don't feel like I have a minute to waste.

Everything we do as leaders affects those we lead, so the fear of my inadequacy as a leader can easily keep me up at night. But a calling isn't meant to be a burden. A calling is meant to be compelling. A calling is the unleashing of all of who we are for God's great good. The weight of responsibility, the fear of inadequacy, and the longing for perfection are all healthy tensions that keep us tethered to our greatest need as leaders: to love the Lord our God with all our heart, with all our soul, with all our mind, and with all our strength.

> **A calling is the unleashing of all of who we are for God's great good.**

Several years ago I decided to add running to my exercise routine. I never considered myself a runner. In fact, going more than a mile or two never felt doable. But after much prompting by my husband, I was convinced I needed to stick with it and see if I had more in me than I thought. For several weeks I did a walk/run rhythm for a two-mile route. I identified sections of the route that I ran and sections that I gave myself permission to walk. Every week I shortened the walking sections, thereby increasing the running sections. It was slow, but it was progress. The first time I completed that two-mile route by running the entire thing, I was elated with an achievement I didn't think I had in me.

But even though I had achieved it, it wasn't easy. I didn't experience the runner's high that real runners speak of. I kept at it, though, adding a half mile every few months. The first time I ran a full five miles, something began to change. I was pretty sure I had finally experienced the runner's high. About three miles in I didn't feel like I was striving. I was running with ease. My breathing was steady and controlled. My legs were fluid and light. I felt like I could run forever. *Runner's World* magazine describes the pace at which this phenomenon occurs as "comfortably challenging."[1]

Leading with our whole self—heart, soul, mind, and strength—is like experiencing that runner's high. It happens when all the dimensions are working fluidly together and you're experiencing progress toward your goal. Like long-distance running, extraordinary leadership can't be achieved without work, focus, discipline, and perseverance. It requires developing muscles that we didn't know we had. It requires committing to regular practice, continuing to engage with our team, pushing ourselves a little further than we're comfortable, and selecting carefully what fuels us and provides energy.

Extraordinary leadership emerges from a commitment deep within us. It's not a fad to follow or a new method to model. Leading with everything we are means putting everything we have on the line for the cause we are compelled by. Heart, soul, mind, and strength leaders know their leadership takes work, engagement, commitment, perseverance, and determination. Much like a runner's high, leadership highs won't happen the first time you exercise your leadership muscle. In fact, you'll lead every day but only feel those moments of effortless joy occasionally. But when you experience them, they keep you going for days and months more.

You are called to be an extraordinary leader. Heart, soul, mind, and strength leadership is possible. God hasn't called you to a place of influence to leave you ill equipped for the responsibility. I still marvel that his formula for leadership is grounded in his instruction for everyone. Love God. Love others. So simple yet so profound.

Philippians 1:6 says, "He who began a good work in you will perfect it until the day of Christ Jesus" (NASB). Perfection isn't a goal to be attained today or tomorrow. It's a lifelong journey that won't be realized until the day we arrive on heaven's doorstep. The pursuit of perfection is the wrong goal because it's more about loving self than loving God and loving others. Extraordinary doesn't mean perfect. Extraordinary means the pursuit of God's Great Commandment. And in the pursuit of leading with all our heart, with all our soul, and with all our strength, the perfecting continues.

May your leadership be an overflow of all of who you are:
heart,
soul,
mind,
strength.

ACKNOWLEDGMENTS

Little did I know that I would be writing this book during one of the biggest seasons of change in my life. Leaving behind seventeen years of community and friendships in Nashville to start anew in the San Francisco Bay Area was more challenging than I ever dreamed. I couldn't find a grocery store let alone find time to write! As a result I had to beg the great team at Nelson Books for extension after extension on my manuscript deadline. Brian Hampton and Kristen Parrish, thank you for generously allowing me the time and space to bring this book to life. I'm grateful for your partnership.

Leading with heart, soul, mind, and strength is a concept that I believe in so deeply, and I couldn't have captured it on paper without the great support of my wonderful agent Shannon Litton. Shannon, thank you for understanding my vision and supporting me every step of the way. Matt Litton (no relation to Shannon) was the editor at large who jumped into this manuscript to provide fresh eyes and insight. Matt, thank you for affirming me as a leadership expert and helping me continue to find my voice in writing. Janene MacIvor and Jennifer Greenstein, thank you for your careful editing and for cleaning up all my misplaced modifiers. Darcie Clemen, the assessment brings this concept to life—thank you! Katy Boatman, Tiffany Sawyer, and the entire Nelson Books marketing team, thank you for your passionate commitment to every release.

So many leaders have inspired me to lead with all of my heart, soul, mind, and strength. Many of them are mentioned throughout this book, and so many more deserve to be noted. To bosses, coworkers, staff members, and friends, thank you for walking this journey of leadership with me.

John and Nancy Ortberg, your commitment to my growth and development is a true gift. Thank you for caring more about who I'm becoming than what I'm producing.

Christine Caine and Alli Worthington, thank you for the opportunity to be a part of Propel. Here's to great days ahead for women who lead!

To my family, thank you for your constant encouragement.

Hilda, I love working with you! Thank you for all your extra support. You know me better than I know myself sometimes.

And to Merlyn, for your constant pep talks and unwavering belief. Thanks for being my team!

NOTES

Introduction

1. Mark Sanborn, "Quotes to Inspire Extraordinary Leadership and Remarkable Performance," Mark Sanborn, accessed January 20, 2015, http://www.marksanborn.com/blog/quotes-to-inspire -extraordinary-leadership-remarkable-performance/.
2. Walter A. Elwell, ed., *Baker Encyclopedia of the Bible* (Grand Rapids, MI: Baker Book House, 1988), s.v. "Shema."

Part 1

1. Paul David Tripp, *Instruments in the Redeemer's Hands: People in Need of Change Helping People in Need of Change* (Phillipsburg, NJ: P&R Publishing, 2002), 18.

Chapter 1: Imagine Extraordinary

1. Jim Rohn quoted in Kevin Kruse, "100 Best Quotes on Leadership," *Leadership* (blog), *Forbes*, October 16, 2012, http:// www.forbes.com/sites/kevinkruse/2012/10/16/quotes-on -leadership/.
2. Steven F. Hayward, *Greatness: Reagan, Churchill & the Making of Extraordinary Leaders* (New York: Three Rivers Press, 2005), 168.

3. Ibid., 166.

4. Kevin Kruse, "What Is Leadership?," *Leadership* (blog), *Forbes*, April 9, 2013, http://www.forbes.com/sites/kevinkruse/2013 /04/09/what-is-leadership/.

5. Lydia Dishman, "The Military Muscle Shaping Yale's Leadership Training," *Fast Company*, July 26, 2012, http://www.fastcompany .com/1843607/military-muscle-shaping-yales-leadership-training.

Chapter 2: Leading in Chaos

1. Brad Lomenick, "Managing Leadership Tensions," Brad Lomenick, December 21, 2010, http://www.bradlomenick.com /2010/12/21/managing-leadership-tensions/.

2. Deepak Chopra, "The Leadership Vacuum—Make It Your Friend," *Huffington Post*, December 27, 2010, http://www.huffingtonpost .com/deepak-chopra/the-leadership-vacuum_b_801516.html.

3. Knowledge@Wharton, "Tylenol and the Legacy of J&J's James Burke," *Time*, October 5, 2012, http://business.time.com/2012 /10/05/tylenol-and-the-legacy-of-jjs-james-burke/.

4. Jim Collins, "The 10 Greatest CEOs of All Time: What These Extraordinary Leaders Can Teach Today's Troubled Executives," *Fortune*, July 21, 2003, http://archive.fortune.com/magazines /fortune/fortune_archive/2003/07/21/346095/index.htm.

5. Mark Miller, *The Heart of Leadership: Becoming a Leader People Want to Follow* (San Francisco: Berrett-Koehler, 2013), 15.

6. John C. Maxwell, "Momentum Breakers vs. Momentum Makers," 2011, http://www.johnmaxwell.com/uploads/general/Momentum _Breakers_vs_Momentum_Makers.pdf.

7. Knowledge@Wharton, "Tylenol and the Legacy of J&J's James Burke."

8. Henry H. Halley, *Halley's Bible Handbook* (Grand Rapids, MI: Zondervan, 2007), 277.

9. Ram Charan, Stephen Drotter, and James Noel, *The Leadership Pipeline: How to Build the Leadership-Powered Company* (San Francisco: Jossey-Bass, 2001), 25.

Chapter 3: Leading from Within

1. Thomas J. Watson quoted in "Model the Way," *Move Me Quotes*, accessed January 20, 2015, http://www.movemequotes.com/tag/model-the-way/.

2. Otto Kroeger, Janet M. Thuesen, and Hile Rutledge, *Type Talk at Work: How the 16 Personality Types Determine Your Success on the Job* (New York: Dell, 2002), 14.

3. Mark Freeman, "Personal Strategies Can Lead to Self-Leadership," *Birmingham Business Journal*, October 10, 2004, http://www.bizjournals.com/birmingham/stories/2004/10/11/focus2.html?page=all.

4. "The Power & Wisdom of the Enneagram," *The Enneagram Institute*, accessed July 20, 2015, http://www.enneagraminstitute.com/.

5. Susan Cain, *Quiet: The Power of Introverts in a World That Can't Stop Talking* (New York: Crown, 2012), 53.

6. Chris Lowney, *Heroic Leadership: Best Practices from a 450-Year-Old Company That Changed the World* (Chicago: Loyola Press, 2003), 27.

7. Pete Scazzero, "Emotionally Healthy Spirituality: Bridging the Counselor/Church Divide," accessed January 20, 2015, http://www.emotionallyhealthy.org/wp-content/uploads/2013/08/bridgingthecounselor.pdf.

8. John Ortberg, Twitter post, December 28, 2012, 5:25 a.m., https://twitter.com/johnortberg.

9. Tommy Newberry, *40 Days to a Joy-Filled Life: Living the 4:8 Principle* (Carol Stream, IL: Tyndale, 2012), 199.

10. "Jim Rohn Quotes," *Brainy Quote*, accessed January 20, 2015, http://www.brainyquote.com/quotes/quotes/j/jimrohn109882.html.

11. John Ortberg, Twitter post, retweeted from Kevin Penry, May 15, 2013, https://twitter.com/johnortberg.

12. Seth Godin, *Tribes: We Need You to Lead Us* (New York: Portfolio, 2008), 55.

13. Henry Blackaby and Richard Blackaby, *Spiritual Leadership: Moving People on to God's Agenda* (Nashville: Broadman & Holman, 2011), 51.

Part 2

1. Bhagwan Shree Rajneesh quoted in "Bhagwan Shree Rajneesh," *Biography.com*, accessed January 9, 2015, http://www.biography .com/people/bhagwan-shree-rajneesh-20900613#later-life.

Chapter 4: Lead with All Your Heart

1. Ralph Waldo Emerson quoted in "Quotes on Relationships," *Leadership Now*, accessed January 20, 2015, http://www .leadershipnow.com/relationshipsquotes.html.

2. Eric Metaxas, *7 Men and the Secret of Their Greatness* (Nashville: Thomas Nelson, 2013), 153.

3. Ibid.

4. John Ortberg, "Everybody's Weird" (blog posting), John Ortberg, March 28, 2014, http://www.johnortberg.com/everybodys-weird/.

5. Simon Sinek, "How Great Leaders Inspire Action," filmed September 2009, TED video, 18:04, http://www.ted.com/talks /simon_sinek_how_great_leaders_inspire_action.html.

6. Tim Sanders, *Love Is The Killer App* (New York: Three Rivers Press, 2002), 3.

7. Ibid., 11.

8. "About Emotional Intelligence," *MHS*, 2011, http://ei.mhs.com /AboutEmotionalIntelligence.aspx.

9. Daniel Goleman, *Working with Emotional Intelligence* (New York: Bantam Books, 1998), 7.

10. Ibid., 8–9.

11. *Merriam-Webster.com*, s.v. "encourage," accessed January 11, 2015, http://www.merriam-webster.com/dictionary/encourage.

12. Dan Rockwell, "10 Ways to Gain Influence," *Leadership Freak* (blog), October 30, 2012, http://leadershipfreak.wordpress.com /2012/10/30/the-10-ways-to-gain-influence/.

13. Stephen M. R. Covey, *The Speed of Trust: The One Thing That Changes Everything* (New York: Free Press, 2006), 1.

14. Ibid., 30.

15. "Best Companies 2014," *Fortune*, accessed January 12, 2015, http://money.cnn.com/magazines/fortune/best-companies/.

16. "Zappos Family Core Values," *Zappos*, accessed January 12, 2015, http://about.zappos.com/our-unique-culture/zappos-core-values.

17. Henry Blackaby and Richard Blackaby, *Spiritual Leadership: Moving People on to God's Agenda* (Nashville: Broadman & Holman, 2011), 13.

18. Ron Johnson quoted in Carmine Gallo, *The Apple Experience: Secrets to Building Insanely Great Customer Loyalty* (New York: McGraw-Hill, 2012), 1.

19. Florence Nightingale quoted in Edward Chaney, "Egypt in England and America: The Cultural Memorials of Religion, Royalty and Revolution," in *Sites of Exchange: European Crossroads and Faultlines*, ed. Maurizio Ascari and Adriana Corrado (Amsterdam: Rodopi, 2006), 39–74.

20. "StrengthsFinder," *StrengthsFinder*, accessed July 20, 2015, strengthsfinder.com.

21. Tommy Newberry, *40 Days to a Joy-Filled Life: Living the 4:8 Principle* (Carol Stream, IL: Tyndale, 2012), 248.

Chapter 5: Lead with All Your Soul

1. Ruth Haley Barton, *Strengthening the Soul of Your Leadership: Seeking God in the Crucible of Ministry* (Downers Grove, IL: InterVarsity Press, 2008), 210.

2. Eric Metaxas, *7 Men and the Secret of Their Greatness* (Nashville: Thomas Nelson, 2013), 101.

3. Eberhard Bethge, *Dietrich Bonhoeffer: Eine Biographie* (Minneapolis: Fortress Press, 2000), 736.

4. Henry Blackaby and Richard Blackaby, *Spiritual Leadership: Moving People on to God's Agenda* (Nashville: Broadman & Holman, 2011), xiv.

5. David Green, "Christian Companies Can't Bow to Sinful Mandate," *USA Today*, September 12, 2012, http://usatoday30.usatoday.com/news/opinion/forum/story/2012-09-12/hhs-mandate-birth-control-sue-hobby-lobby/57759226/1.

6. "Forbes 100: David Green," *Forbes*, accessed January 12, 2015, http://www.forbes.com/profile/david-green/.

7. Green, "Christian Companies."

8. Ibid.

9. Ibid.

10. Brother Lawrence, *The Brother Lawrence Collection* (Radford, VA: Wilder Publications, 2008), 56.

11. Obed Martinez, speech at Young Pastors Gathering at Saddleback Church, Lake Forest, California, February 21, 2014.

12. Henry H. Halley, *Halley's Bible Handbook* (Grand Rapids, MI: Zondervan, 2007), 321.

13. Adam Grant, *Give and Take: A Revolutionary Approach to Success* (New York: Viking, 2013), excerpted at *Psychology Today* (blog), accessed January 13, 2015, http://www.psychologytoday.com /blog/give-and-take/201308/how-think-wise-person.

14. Ibid.

15. "About the Study," *SoulPulse*, accessed January 13, 2015, http:// soulpulse.org/#call-to-action.

16. Richard J. Foster, *Prayer: Finding the Heart's True Home* (San Francisco: Harper San Francisco, 1992), 191.

17. "Ken Blanchard Quotations," *Ideas and Training*, accessed January 13, 2015, http://www.ideasandtraining.com/Ken-Blanchard-Quotations.html.

18. Albert Schweitzer quoted in "Set the Example," *Move Me Quotes*, accessed January 13, 2015, http://www.movemequotes.com/tag /set-the-example/.

19. Bill Hybels, *Too Busy Not to Pray* (Downers Grove, IL: InterVarsity Press, 2008), 119.

Chapter 6: Lead with All Your Mind

1. "About Dr. Leaf," Dr. Caroline Leaf, accessed January 13, 2015, http://drleaf.com/about/.

2. Caroline Leaf, *Switch On Your Brain: The Key to Peak Happiness, Thinking, and Health* (Grand Rapids, MI: Baker Books, 2013), 20.

3. Jim Collins, *Good to Great: Why Some Companies Make the Leap . . . and Others Don't* (New York: Harper Business, 2001), chapter 8.

4. *Dictionary.com*, s.v. "manage," accessed January 13, 2015, http://dictionary.reference.com/browse/Manage?s=t.

5. Simon Sinek, *Start with Why: How Great Leaders Inspire Everyone to Take Action* (New York: Portfolio, 2009), 67.

6. Jim Collins and Morten T. Hansen, *Great by Choice: Uncertainty, Chaos, and Luck—Why Some Thrive Despite Them All* (New York: Harper Business, 2011), chapters 2–3.

7. David Allen, *Getting Things Done: The Art of Stress-Free Productivity* (New York: Penguin Books, 2001), 18–19.

8. Simon Sinek, "How Great Leaders Inspire Action," filmed September 2009, TED video, 18:04, http://www.ted.com/talks/simon_sinek_how_great_leaders_inspire_action.html.

9. Joseph George, "Organizational Alignment: Don't Overlook This Key to Success," *Forbes* BrandVoice, January 30, 2014, http://www.forbes.com/sites/sungardas/2014/01/30/organizational-alignment-dont-overlook-this-key-to-success/.

10. Rudolph W. Giuliani, *Leadership* (New York: Hyperion, 2002), 70.

11. John C. Maxwell, *Everyone Communicates, Few Connect: What the Most Effective People Do Differently* (Nashville: Thomas Nelson, 2010), 159.

12. Ken Robinson, *Out of Our Minds: Learning to Be Creative*, 2nd ed. (Bloomington, MN: Capstone Publishing, 2011), x.

Chapter 7: Lead with All Your Strength

1. Malcolm Gladwell quoted in "Visionary Quotes," *Brainy Quote*, accessed January 13, 2015, http://www.brainyquote.com/quotes/keywords/visionary.html#gF6hef2mFs4OfVj2.99.

2. Bill Hybels, speech at The Global Leadership Summit, South Barrington, IL, August 8–9, 2013; notes from the speech can be found at http://www.jennicatron.com/the-courage-that-leadership-requires-bill-hybels/.

3. Christine Caine, "Vision," *Coffee with Christ*, podcast audio, May 5,

2014, http://www.christinecaine.com/content/podcasts/gjeqgo
?permcode=gjeqgo&page=7#.VLcFsyd9uVp.

4. "Katie's Story," *Azima Ministries*, accessed January 13, 2015, http://
www.amazima.org/katiesstory.html.

5. Scott Harrison, "Scott's Story," Charity: Water, accessed January
15, 2015, http://www.charitywater.org/about/scotts_story.php.

6. Dan Schawbel, "Scott Harrison: How He Started charity: water
and What He Learned in the Process," *Entrepreneurs* (blog), *Forbes*,
July 22, 2013, http://www.forbes.com/sites/danschawbel/2013/07
/22/scott-harrison-how-he-started-charity-water-and-what-he
-learned-in-the-process/.

7. Carmine Gallo, *The Apple Experience: Secrets to Building Insanely
Great Customer Loyalty* (New York: McGraw-Hill, 2012), 3.

8. Ibid.

9. Leon Neyfakh, "The Myth of the Visionary Leader," *Boston Globe*,
October 20, 2013, http://www.bostonglobe.com/ideas/2013/10/20
/the-myth-visionary-leader/zyQGpoehGxugSIivN1a8pN/story
.html.

10. Mark Miller, *The Heart of Leadership: Becoming a Leader People Want
to Follow* (San Francisco: Berrett-Koehler, 2013), 81.

11. Nathaniel Koloc, "What Job Candidates Really Want: Meaningful
Work," *Harvard Business Review*, April 18, 2013, https://hbr.org
/2013/04/what-job-candidates-really-wan/.

12. "Team charity: water," Charity: Water, accessed January 15, 2015,
http://www.charitywater.org/about/.

13. Nick Bilton, "One on One: Scott Harrison, Charity Water," *Bits*
(blog), *New York Times*, January 2, 2012, http://bits.blogs.nytimes
.com/2012/01/02/one-on-one-scott-harrison-charity-water/?_r=0.

14. Chris McChesney, Sean Covey, and Jim Huling, *The 4 Disciplines
of Execution: Achieving Your Wildly Important Goals* (New York: Free
Press, 2012), 7.

15. Seth Godin, *Tribes: We Need You to Lead Us* (New York: Penguin
Books, 2008), 108.

Part 3

1. James M. Kouzes and Barry Z. Posner, *The Leadership Challenge*, 4th ed. (San Francisco: John Wiley & Sons, 2007), xii.

Chapter 8: Putting Extraordinary into Practice

1. Kenneth E. Strong and John A. DiCicco, *Leadership Is a Choice: Conquer Your Fears and Make the Decision to Lead* (Mustang, OK: Tate, 2010), 178.

2. Jesse Jackson quoted in Simran Khurana, "Leadership Quotes," *About.com*, accessed January 15, 2015, http://quotations.about .com/od/inspirationquotes/a/leadership.htm.

3. "How Strengths Become Weaknesses," *Bloomberg Businessweek*, December 20, 2005, http://www.businessweek.com/stories/2005 –12–20/how-strengths-become-weaknesses.

4. "Harvey S. Firestone Quotes," *BrainyQuote*, accessed January 15, 2015, http://www.brainyquote.com/quotes/quotes/h/harveysfi158289.html.

5. Sam Walton quoted in Simran Khurana, "Motivation and Leadership Quotes," About.com, accessed January 15, 2015, http:// quotations.about.com/cs/inspirationquotes/a/Leadership12.htm.

6. For one of the studies, see Bureau of Labor Statistics, U.S. Department of Labor, "Number of Jobs Held, Labor Market Activity, and Earnings Growth Among the Youngest Baby Boomers: Results from a Longitudinal Study," news release, July 25, 2012, http://www.bls.gov/news.release/pdf/nlsoy.pdf.

Epilogue: You Were Born to Be Extraordinary

1. K. Aleisha Fetters, "How to Achieve a Runner's High," *Runner's World*, April 25, 2014, http://www.runnersworld.com/running -tips/how-to-achieve-a-runners-high.

ABOUT THE AUTHOR

Jenni Catron is a writer, speaker, and leadership coach who consults churches and non-profits to help them lead from their extraordinary best. Her passion is to lead well and to inspire, equip and encourage others to do the same. She speaks at conferences and churches nationwide, seeking to help others develop their leadership gifts and lead confidently in the different spheres of influence God has granted them. Additionally, she consults with individuals and teams on leadership and organizational health.

Jenni blogs at www.jennicatron.com and contributes to a number of other online publications as well. *Outreach Magazine* has recognized her as one of the thirty emerging influencers reshaping church leadership

A leader who loves "putting feet to vision," Jenni served on the executive leadership teams of Menlo Church in Menlo Park, California, and Cross Point Church in Nashville, Tennessee. Prior to ministry leadership, she worked as an Artist Development Director in the Christian music industry.

Jenni loves a fabulous cup of tea, great books, learning the game of tennis, and hanging out with her husband and their border collie.

WANT TO SEE YOUR TEAM GROW IN THE 4 DIMENSIONS OF EXTRAORDINARY LEADERSHIP?

Visit **jennicatron.com** for more information about
The 4 Dimensions of Extraordinary Leadership Team Kit designed to:

- Lead your staff, department, executive team, or volunteer group in a better understanding of leading from your heart, soul, mind, and strength
- Assess each team member on his or her strong dimensions and how they impact the organization
- Help the team understand how to lead collaboratively in the four dimensions

WANT TO
TAKE IT A
STEP
FURTHER?

- Book Jenni to lead a training day or retreat with your staff
- Host an Extraordinary Leader event at your church or organization

Go to **jennicatron.com** for more details!

BLOG: JenniCatron.com
TWITTER: @JenniCatron
  (Tag your tweet with #ExtraordinaryLeadership.)
FACEBOOK: Facebook.com/authorjennicatron
INSTAGRAM: JenniCatron